M. BUTTERFLY

BY DAVID HENRY HWANG

★

★

**DRAMATISTS
PLAY SERVICE
INC.**

ABOUT THE AUTHOR

Born in 1957, David Henry Hwang, the son of first-generation Chinese-Americans, grew up in California and currently makes his home in Los Angeles. His play *FOB*, originally staged at Stanford University during his senior year there, was further developed at the O'Neill Playwrights Conference and presented at the New York Shakespeare Festival's Public Theater in 1980. *The Dance and the Railroad, Family Devotions* and a pair of one-acts — *The House of Sleeping Beauties* and *The Sound of a Voice* — were also produced at the Public. *Rich Relations* premiered at New York's Second Stage in 1986. Hwang's current project is *1000 Airplanes on the Roof*, a science-fiction musical drama created with composer Philip Glass and designer Jerome Sirlin, which is scheduled to open this month in Vienna, the first stage of an international tour.

FOB was chosen for publication in TCG's *New Plays USA 1* anthology, and later included in *Broken Promises*, an anthology of Hwang's plays published by Avon Books. The recipient of an Obie and a CINE Golden Eagle, as well as Guggenheim, Rockefeller and NYSCA fellowships, Hwang this year was awarded a two-year fellowship by the National Endowment for the Arts.

PLAYWRIGHT'S NOTES
A former French diplomat and a Chinese opera singer have been sentenced to six years in jail for spying for China after a two-day trial that traced a story of clandestine love and mistaken sexual identity. . . .

Mr. Bouriscot was accused of passing information to China after he fell in love with Mr. Shi, whom he believed for twenty years to be a woman.

—*The New York Times*,
May 11, 1986

This play was suggested by international newspaper accounts of a recent espionage trial. For purposes of dramatization, names have been changed, characters created, and incidents devised or altered, and this play does not purport to be a factual record of real events or real people.

I could escape this feeling
With my China girl . . .

—David Bowie & Iggy Pop

M. BUTTERFLY premiered on February 10, 1988 at Washington, D.C.'s National Theatre, in a production directed by John Dexter. Moving to Broadway, the production opened March 20, 1988 at the Eugene O'Neill Theatre. The scenery and costumes were by Eiko Ishioka, lighting by Andy Phillips, hair by Phyllis Della, music by Giacomo Puccini and Lucia Hwong with Peking Opera consultants Jamie H.J. Guan and Michele Ehlers. The production stage manager was Bob Borod, and the cast was as follows:

Rene Gallimard . . . . John Lithgow
Song Liling . . . . B. D. Wong
Marc/Man #2/Consul Sharpless . . . . John Getz
Renee/Woman at Party/Girl in Magazine . Lindsay Frost
Comrade Chin/Suzuki/Shu-Fang . . . . . . Lori Tan Chinn
Helga . . . . Rose Gregorio
M. Toulon/Man #1/Judge . . . . George N. Martin
Kurogo Dancers . . . . . Alec Mapa, Chris Odo, H. J. Guan

M. BUTTERFLY won the Tony for best play, the Outer Critics Circle Award for best Broadway play, the John Gassner Award for best American play, and the Drama Desk Award for best new play.

TIME AND PLACE
The action of the play takes place in a Paris prison in the present, and, in recall, during the decade 1960 – 70 in Beijing, and from 1966 to the present in Paris.

M. BUTTERFLY

ACT ONE

SCENE 1

M. Gallimard's prison cell. Paris, 1988.

Lights fade up to reveal Rene Gallimard, 65, in a prison cell. He wears a comfortable bathrobe, and looks old and tired. The sparsely furnished cell contains a wooden crate upon which sits a hot plate with a kettle, and a portable tape recorder. Gallimard sits on the crate staring at the recorder, a sad smile on his face.

Upstage Song, who appears as a beautiful woman in traditional Chinese garb, dances a traditional piece from the Peking Opera, surrounded by the percussive clatter of Chinese music.

Then, slowly, lights and sound cross-fade; the Chinese opera music dissolves into a Western opera, the "Love Duet" from Puccini's Madame Butterfly.* *Song continues dancing, now to the Western accompaniment. Though her movements are the same, the difference in music now gives them a balletic quality.*

Gallimard rises, and turns U.S. *towards the figure of Song, who dances without acknowledging him.*

GALLIMARD. Butterfly, Butterfly . . . (*He forces himself to turn away, as the image of Song fades out, and talks to us.*) The limits of my cell are as such: four-and-a-half meters by five. There's one window against the far wall; a door, very strong, to protect me from autograph hounds. I'm responsible for

---

* See Special Note on Copyright page

the tape recorder, the hot plate, and this charming coffee table.

When I want to eat, I'm marched off to the dining room — hot, steaming slop appears on my plate. When I want to sleep, the light bulb turns itself off — the work of fairies. It's an enchanted space I occupy. The French — we know how to run a prison.

But, to be honest, I'm not treated like an ordinary prisoner. Why? Because I'm a celebrity. You see, I make people laugh.

I never dreamed this day would arrive. I've never been considered witty or clever. In fact, as a young boy, in an informal poll among my grammar school classmates, I was voted "least likely to be invited to a party." It's a title I managed to hold onto for many years. Despite some stiff competition.

But now, how the tables turn! Look at me: the life of every social function in Paris. Paris? Why be modest? My fame has spread to Amsterdam, London, New York. Listen to them! In the world's smartest parlors. I'm the one who lifts their spirits! (*With a flourish, Gallimard directs our attention to another part of the stage.*)

SCENE 2

A party. 1988.
Lights go up on a chic-looking parlor, where a well-dressed trio, two men and one woman, make conversation. Gallimard also remains lit; he observes them from his cell.

WOMAN. And what of Gallimard?
MAN 1. Gallimard?
MAN 2. Gallimard!
GALLIMARD. (*To us.*) You see? They're all determined to say my name, as if it were some new dance.
WOMAN. He still claims not to believe the truth.
MAN 1. What? Still? Even since the trial?
WOMAN. Yes. Isn't it mad?

MAN 2. (*Laughing.*) He says . . . it was dark . . . and she was very modest! (*The trio break into laughter.*)

MAN 1. So — what? He never touched her with his hands?

MAN 2. Perhaps he did, and simply misidentified the equipment. A compelling case for sex education in the schools.

WOMAN. To protect the National Security — the Church can't argue with that.

MAN 1. That's impossible! How could he not know?

MAN 2. Simple ignorance.

MAN 1. For twenty years?

MAN 2. Time flies when you're being stupid.

WOMAN. Well, I thought the French were ladies' men.

MAN 2. It seems Monsieur Gallimard was overly anxious to live up to his national reputation.

WOMAN. Well, he's not very good-looking.

MAN 1. No, he's not.

MAN 2. Certainly not.

WOMAN. Actually, I feel sorry for him.

MAN 2. A toast! To Monsieur Gallimard!

WOMAN. Yes! to Gallimard!

MAN 1. To Gallimard!

MAN 2. Vive la différence! (*They toast, laughing. Lights down on them.*)

SCENE 3

M. Gallimard's cell.

GALLIMARD. (*Smiling.*) You see? They toast me. I've become patron saint of the socially inept. Can they really be so foolish? Men like that — they should be scratching at my door, begging to learn my secrets! For I, Rene Gallimard, you see, I have known, and been loved by . . . the Perfect Woman.

Alone in this cell, I sit night after night, watching our story play through my head, always searching for a new ending, one which redeems my honor, where she returns at last to my arms. And I imagine you — my ideal audience — who come to understand and even, perhaps just a little, to envy me. (*He turns on his tape recorder. Over the house speakers, we hear the opening phrases of* Madame Butterfly.) In order for you to understand what I did and why, I must introduce you to my favorite opera: *Madame Butterfly*. By Giacomo Puccini. First produced at La Scala, Milan, in 1904, it is now beloved throughout the Western world. (*As Gallimard describes the opera, the tape segues in and out to sections he may be describing.*) And why not? Its heroine, Cio-Cio-San, also known as Butterfly, is a feminine ideal, beautiful and brave. And its hero, the man for whom she gives up everything, is — (*He pulls out a naval officer's cap from under his crate, pops it on his head, and struts about.*) — not very good-looking, not too bright, and pretty much a wimp: Benjamin Franklin Pinkerton of the U.S. Navy. As the curtain rises, he's just closed on two great bargains: one on a house, the other on a woman — call it a package deal.

Pinkerton purchased the rights to Butterfly for one hundred yen — in modern currency, equivalent to about . . . sixty-six cents. So, he's feeling pretty pleased with himself as Sharpless, the American consul, arrives to witness the marriage. (*Marc, wearing an official cap to designate Sharpless, Enters and plays the character.*)

SHARPLESS/MARC. Pinkerton!

PINKERTON/GALLIMARD. Sharpless! How's it hangin'? It's a great day, just great. Between my house, my wife, and the rickshaw ride in from town, I've saved nineteen cents just this morning.

SHARPLESS. Wonderful. I can see the inscription on your tombstone already: "I saved a dollar, here I lie." (*He looks around.*) Nice house.

PINKERTON. It's artistic. Artistic, don't you think? Like the way the shoji screens slide open to reveal the wet bar and disco mirror ball? Classy, huh? Great for impressing the chicks.

SHARPLESS. "Chicks"? Pinkerton, you're going to be a married man!

PINKERTON. Well, sort of.

SHARPLESS. What do you mean?

PINKERTON. This country — Sharpless, it is okay. You got all these geisha girls running around —
SHARPLESS. I know! I live here!
PINKERTON. Then, you know the marriage laws, right? I split for one month, it's annulled!
SHARPLESS. Leave it to you to read the fine print. Who's the lucky girl?
PINKERTON. Cio-Cio-San. Her friends call her Butterfly. Sharpless, she eats out of my hand!
SHARPLESS. She's probably very hungry.
PINKERTON. Not like American girls. It's true what they say about Oriental girls. They want to be treated bad!
SHARPLESS. Oh, please!
PINKERTON. It's true!
SHARPLESS. Are you serious about this girl?
PINKERTON. I'm marrying her, aren't I?
SHARPLESS. Yes — with generous trade-in terms.
PINKERTON. When I leave, she'll know what it's like to have loved a real man. And I'll even buy her a few nylons.
SHARPLESS. You aren't planning to take her with you?
PINKERTON. Huh? Where?
SHARPLESS. Home!
PINKERTON. You mean, America? Are you crazy? Can you see her trying to buy rice in St. Louis?
SHARPLESS. So, you're not serious. (*Pause.*)
PINKERTON/GALLIMARD. (*as Pinkerton*) Consul, I am a sailor in port. (*As Gallimard.*) They then proceed to sing the famous duet, "The Whole World Over." (*The duet plays on the speakers. Gallimard, as Pinkerton, lip-syncs his lines from the opera.*) To give a rough translation: "The whole world over, the Yankee travels, casting his anchor wherever he wants. Life's not worth living unless he can win the hearts of the fairest maidens, then hotfoot it off the premises ASAP." (*He turns towards Marc.*) In the preceding scene, I played Pinkerton, the womanizing cad, and my friend Marc from school . . . (*Marc bows grandly for our benefit.*) played Sharpless, the sensitive soul of reason. In life, however, our positions were usually — no, always — reversed.

Scene 4

Ecole Nationale, Aix-en-Provence. 1947.

GALLIMARD. No, Marc, I think I'd rather stay home.

MARC. Are you crazy?! We are going to Dad's condo in Marseille! You know what happened last time?

GALLIMARD. Of course I do.

MARC. Of course you don't! You never know . . . They stripped, Rene!

GALLIMARD. Who stripped?

MARC. The girls!

GALLIMARD. Girls? Who said anything about girls?

MARC. Rene, we're a buncha university guys goin' up to the woods. What are we gonna do—talk philosophy?

GALLIMARD. What girls? Where do you get them?

MARC. Who cares? The point is, they come. On trucks. Packed in like sardines. The back flips open, babes hop out, we're ready to roll.

GALLIMARD. You mean, they just—?

MARC. Before you know it, every last one of them—they're stripped and splashing around my pool. There's no moon out, they can't see what's going on, their boobs are flapping, right? You close your eyes, reach out—it's grab bag, get it? Doesn't matter whose ass is between whose legs, whose teeth are sinking into who. You're just in there, going at it, eyes closed, on and on for as long as you can stand. (*Pause.*) Some fun, huh?

GALLIMARD. What happens in the morning?

MARC. In the morning, you're ready to talk some philosophy. (*Beat.*) So how 'bout it?

GALLIMARD. Marc, I can't . . . I'm afraid they'll say no —the girls. So I never ask.

MARC. You don't have to ask! That's the beauty—don't you see? They don't have to say yes. It's perfect for a guy like you, really.

GALLIMARD. You go ahead . . . I may come later.

MARC. Hey, Rene—it doesn't matter that you're clumsy and got zits—they're not looking!

GALLIMARD. Thank you very much.

MARC. Wimp. (*Marc walks over to the other side of the stage, and starts waving and smiling at women in the audience.*)

GALLIMARD. (*To us.*) We now return to my version of *Madame Butterfly* and the events leading to my recent conviction for treason. (*Gallimard notices Marc making lewd gestures.*) Marc, what are you doing?

MARC. Huh? (*Sotto voce.*) Rene, there're a lotta great babes out there. They're probably lookin' at me and thinking, "What a dangerous guy."

GALLIMARD. Yes — how could they help but be impressed by your cool sophistication? (*Gallimard pops the Sharpless cap on Marc's head, and points him offstage, Marc Exits, leering.*)

SCENE 5

M. Gallimard's cell.

GALLIMARD. Next, Butterfly makes her entrance. We learn her age — fifteen . . . but very mature for her years. (*Lights come up on the area where we saw Song dancing at the top of the play. She appears there again, now dressed as Madame Butterfly, moving to the "Love Duet." Gallimard turns U.S. slightly to watch, transfixed.*) But as she glides past him, beautiful, laughing softly behind her fan, don't we who are men sigh with hope? We, who are not handsome, nor brave, nor powerful, yet somehow believe, like Pinkerton, that we deserve a Butterfly. She arrives with all her possessions in the folds of her sleeves, lays them all out, for her man to do with as he pleases. Even her life itself — she bows her head as she whispers that she's not even worth the hundred yen he paid for her. He's already given too much, when we know he's really had to give nothing at all. (*Music and lights on Song out. Gallimard sits at his crate.*) In real life, women who put their total worth at less than sixty-six cents are quite hard to find. The closest we come is in the pages of these magazines. (*He reaches into his crate, pulls out a stack of girlie magazines, and begins flipping through them.*) Quite a necessity in prison. For three or four dollars, you get seven or eight women.

13

I first discovered these magazines at my uncle's house. One day, as a boy of twelve. The first time I saw them in his closet . . . all lined up — my body shook. Not with lust — no, with power. Here were women — a shelfful — who would do exactly as I wanted. (*The "Love Duet" creeps in over the speakers. Special comes up, revealing, not Song this time, but a pinup girl in a sexy negligee, her back to us. Gallimard turns* U.S. *and looks at her.*)

GIRL. I know you're watching me.

GALLIMARD. My throat . . . it's dry.

GIRL. I leave my blinds open every night before I go to bed.

GALLIMARD. I can't move.

GIRL. I leave my blinds open and the lights on.

GALLIMARD. I'm shaking. My skin is hot, but my penis is soft. Why?

GIRL. I stand in front of the window.

GALLIMARD. What is she going to do?

GIRL. I toss my hair, and I let my lips part . . . barely.

GALLIMARD. I shouldn't be seeing this. It's so dirty. I'm so bad.

GIRL. Then, slowly, I lift off my nightdress.

GALLIMARD. Oh, god. I can't believe it. I can't —

GIRL. I toss it to the ground.

GALLIMARD. Now, she's going to walk away. She's going to —

GIRL. I stand there, in the light, displaying myself.

GALLIMARD. No. She's — why is she naked?

GIRL. To you.

GALLIMARD. In front of a window? This is wrong. No —

GIRL. Without shame.

GALLIMARD. No, she must . . . like it.

GIRL. I like it.

GALLIMARD. She . . . she wants me to see.

GIRL. I want you to see.

GALLIMARD. I can't believe it! She's getting excited!

GIRL. I can't see you. You can do whatever you want.

GALLIMARD. I can't do a thing. Why?

GIRL. What would you like me to do . . . next? (*Lights go down on her. Music off. Silence, as Gallimard puts away his magazines. Then he resumes talking to us.*)

GALLIMARD. Act Two begins with Butterfly staring at the ocean. Pinkerton's been called back to the U.S., and he's given his wife a detailed schedule of his plans. In the column marked "return date," he's written "when the robins nest." This failed to ignite her suspicions. Now, three years have passed without a peep from him. Which brings a response from her faithful servant, Suzuki. (*Comrade Chin enters, playing Suzuki.*)

SUZUKI. Girl, he's a loser. What'd he ever give you? Nineteen cents and those ugly Day-Glo stockings? Look, it's finished! Kaput! Done! And you should be glad! I mean, the guy was a woofer! He tried before, you know — before he met you, he went down to geisha central and plunked down his spare change in front of the usual candidates — everyone else gagged! These are hungry prostitutes, and they were not interested, get the picture? Now, stop slathering when an American ship sails in, and let's make some bucks — I mean, yen! We are broke!

Now, what about Yamadori? Hey, hey — don't look away — the man is a prince — figuratively, and, what's even better, literally. He's rich, he's handsome, he says he'll die if you don't marry him — and he's even willing to overlook the little fact that you've been deflowered all over the place by a foreign devil. What do you mean, "But he's Japanese?" What do you think you are? You think you've been touched by the whitey god? He was a sailor with dirty hands! (*Suzuki stalks offstage.*)

GALLIMARD. She's also visited by Consul Sharpless, sent by Pinkerton on a minor errand. (*Marc enters, as Sharpless.*)

SHARPLESS. I hate this job.

GALLIMARD. This Pinkerton — he doesn't show up personally to tell his wife he's abandoning her. No, he sends a government diplomat . . . at taxpayer's expense.

SHARPLESS. Butterfly? Butterfly? I have some bad — I'm going to be ill. Butterfly, I came to tell you —

GALLIMARD. Butterfly says she knows he'll return and if he doesn't she'll kill herself rather than go back to her own people. (*Beat.*) This causes a lull in the conversation.

SHARPLESS. Let's put it this way . . .

GALLIMARD. Butterfly runs into the next room, and returns holding — (*Sound cue: a baby crying. Sharpless, "seeing" this, backs away.*)

SHARPLESS. Well, good. Happy to see things going so well. I suppose I'll be going now. Ta ta. Ciao. (*He turns away. Sound cue out.*) I hate this job. (*He exits.*)

GALLIMARD. At that moment, Butterfly spots in the harbor an American ship — the *Abramo Lincoln!* (*Music cue: "The Flower Duet." Song, still dressed as Butterfly, changes into a wedding kimono, moving to the music.*) This is the moment that redeems her years of waiting. With Suzuki's help, they cover the room with flowers — (*Chin, as Suzuki, trudges onstage and drops a lone flower without much enthusiasm.*) — and she changes into her wedding dress to prepare for Pinkerton's arrival. (*Suzuki helps Butterfly change. Helga Enters, and helps Gallimard change into a tuxedo.*) I married a woman older than myself — Helga.

HELGA. My father was ambassador to Australia. I grew up among criminals and kangaroos.

GALLIMARD. Hearing that brought me to the altar — (*Helga exits.*) — where I took a vow renouncing love. No fantasy woman would ever want me, so, yes, I would settle for a quick leap up the career ladder. Passion, I banish, and in its place — practicality!

But my vows had long since lost their charm by the time we arrived in China. The sad truth is that all men want a beautiful woman, and the uglier the man, the greater the want. (*Suzuki makes final adjustments of Butterfly's costume, as does Gallimard of his tuxedo.*) I married late, at age thirty-one. I was faithful to my marriage for eight years. Until the day when, as a junior-level diplomat in puritanical Peking, in a parlor at the German ambassador's house, during the "Reign of a Hundred Flowers," I first saw her . . . singing the death scene from *Madame Butterfly.* (*Suzuki runs offstage.*)

SCENE 6

German ambassador's house. Beijing. 1960.
The U.S. *special area now becomes a stage. Several chairs face* U.S., *representing seating for some twenty*

guests in the parlor. A few "diplomats"—Renee, Marc, Toulon—in formal dress Enter and take seats.

Gallimard also sits down, but turns towards us and continues to talk. Orchestral accompaniment on the tape is now replaced by a simple piano. Song picks up the death scene from the point where Butterfly uncovers the hara-kiri knife.

GALLIMARD. The ending is pitiful. Pinkerton, in an act of great courage, stays home and sends his American wife to pick up Butterfly's child. The truth, long deferred, has come up to her door. (*Song, playing Butterfly, sings the lines from the opera in her own voice—which, though not classical, should be decent.*)

SONG. "Con onor muore/ chi non puo serbar/ vita con onore."

GALLIMARD. (*Simultaneously.*) "Death with honor/ Is better than life/ Life with dishonor." (*The stage is illuminated; we are now completely within an elegant diplomat's residence. Song proceeds to play out an abbreviated death scene. Everyone in the room applauds. Song, shyly, takes her bows. Others in the room rush to congratulate her. Gallimard remains with us.*) They say in opera the voice is everything. That's probably why I'd never before enjoyed opera. Here . . . here was a Butterfly with little or no voice—but she had the grace, the delicacy . . . I believed this girl. I believed her suffering. I wanted to take her in my arms—so delicate, even I could protect her, take her home, pamper her until she smiled. (*Over the course of the preceding speech, Song has broken from the U.S. crowd and moved directly upstage of Gallimard.*)

SONG. Excuse me. Monsieur . . . ? (*Gallimard turns U.S., shocked.*)

GALLIMARD. Oh! Gallimard. Mademoiselle . . . ? A beautiful . . .

SONG. Song Liling.

GALLIMARD. A beautiful performance.

SONG. Oh, please.

GALLIMARD. I usually—

SONG. You make me blush. I'm no opera singer at all.

GALLIMARD. I usually don't like *Butterfly*.

SONG. I can't blame you in the least.

GALLIMARD. I mean, the story —

SONG. Ridiculous.

GALLIMARD. I like the story, but . . . what?

SONG. Oh, you like it?

GALLIMARD. I . . . what I mean is, I've always seen it played by huge women in so much bad makeup.

SONG. Bad makeup is not unique to the West.

GALLIMARD. But, who can believe them!

SONG. And you believe me?

GALLIMARD. Absolutely. You were utterly convincing. It's the first time —

SONG. Convincing? As a Japanese woman? The Japanese used hundreds of our people for medical experiments during the war, you know. But I gather such an irony is lost on you.

GALLIMARD. No! I was about to say, it's the first time I've seen the beauty of the story.

SONG. Really?

GALLIMARD. Of her death. It's a . . . a pure sacrifice. He's unworthy, but what can she do? She loves him . . . so much. It's a very beautiful story.

SONG. Well, yes, to a Westerner.

GALLIMARD. Excuse me?

SONG. It's one of your favorite fantasies, isn't it? the submissive Oriental woman and the cruel white man.

GALLIMARD. Well, I didn't quite mean . . .

SONG. Consider it this way: what would you say if a blonde homecoming queen fell in love with a short Japanese businessman? He treats here cruelly, then goes home for three years, during which time she prays to his picture and turns down marriage from a young Kennedy. Then, when she learns he has remarried, she kills herself. Now, I believe you would consider this girl to be a deranged idiot, correct? But because it's an Oriental who kills herself for a Westerner — ah! — you find it beautiful. (*Silence.*)

GALLIMARD. Yes . . . well . . . I see your point . . .

SONG. I will never do Butterfly again, Monsieur Gallimard. If you wish to see some real theatre, come to the Peking

Opera sometime. Expand your mind. (*Song walks offstage. Other guests exit with her.*)

GALLIMARD. (*To us.*) So much for protecting her in my big Western arms.

SCENE 7

M. Gallimard's apartment. Beijing. 1960.
   Gallimard changes from his tux into a casual suit. Helga Enters.

GALLIMARD. The Chinese are an incredibly arrogant people.

HELGA. They warned us about that in Paris, remember?

GALLIMARD. Even Parisians consider them arrogant. That's a switch.

HELGA. What is it that Madame Su says? "We are a very old civilization." I never know if she's talking about her country or herself.

GALLIMARD. I walk around here, all I hear every day, everywhere is how *old* this culture is. The fact that "old" may be synonymous with "senile" doesn't occur to them.

HELGA. You're not going to change them. "East is east, west is west, and . . . " whatever that guy said.

GALLIMARD. It's just that — silly. I met . . . at Ambassador Koening's tonight — you should've been there.

HELGA. Koening? Oh god, no. Did he enchant you all again with the history of Bavaria?

GALLIMARD. No. I met, I suppose, the Chinese equivalent of a diva. She's an singer in the Chinese opera.

HELGA. They have an opera, too? Do they sing in Chinese? Or maybe — in Italian?

GALLIMARD. Tonight, she did sing in Italian.

HELGA. How'd she manage that?

GALLIMARD. She must've been educated in the West before the Revolution. Her French is very good also. Anyway, she sang the death scene from *Madame Butterfly*.

HELGA. *Madame Butterfly*! Then I should have come. (*She*

19

begins humming, floating around the room as if dragging long kimono sleeves.) Did she have a nice costume? I think it's a classic piece of music.

GALLIMARD. That's what *I* thought, too. Don't let her hear you say that.

HELGA. What's wrong?

GALLIMARD. Evidently the Chinese hate it.

HELGA. She hated it, but she performed it anyway? Is she perverse?

GALLIMARD. They hate it because the white man gets the girl. Sour grapes if you ask me.

HELGA. Politics again? Why can't they just hear it as a piece of beautiful music? So, what's in their opera?

GALLIMARD. I don't know. But, whatever it is, I'm sure it must be *old*. (*Helga exits.*)

SCENE 8

Chinese opera house and the streets of Beijing. 1960.
The sound of gongs clanging fills the stage.

GALLIMARD. My wife's innocent question kept ringing in my ears. I asked around, but no one knew anything about the Chinese opera. It took four weeks, but my curiosity overcame my cowardice. This Chinese diva—this unwilling Butterfly—what did she do to make her so proud?

The room was hot, and full of smoke. Wrinkled faces, old women, teeth missing—a man with a growth on his neck, like a human toad. All smiling, pipes falling from their mouths, cracking nuts between their teeth, a live chicken pecking at my foot—all looking, screaming, gawking . . . at her. (*The* U.S. *area is suddenly hit with a harsh white light. It has become the stage for the Chinese opera performance. Two dancers enter, along with Song. Gallimard stands apart, watching. Song glides gracefully amidst the two dancers. Drums suddenly slam to a halt. Song strikes a pose, looking straight at Gallimard. Dancers exit. Light change. Pause, then Song walks right off the stage and straight up to Gallimard.*)

SONG. Yes. You. White man. I'm looking straight at you.

GALLIMARD. Me?

SONG. You see any other white men? It was too easy to spot you. How often does a man in my audience come in a tie? (*Song starts to remove her costume. Underneath, she wears simple baggy clothes. They are now backstage. The show is over.*) So, you are an adventurous imperialist?

GALLIMARD. I . . . thought it would further my education.

SONG. It took you four weeks. Why?

GALLIMARD. I've been busy.

SONG. Well, education has always been undervalued in the West, hasn't it?

GALLIMARD. (*Laughing.*) I don't think that's true.

SONG. No, you wouldn't. You're a Westerner. How can you objectively judge your own values?

GALLIMARD. I think it's possible to achieve some distance.

SONG. Do you? (*Pause.*) It stinks in here. Let's go.

GALLIMARD. These are the smells of your loyal fans.

SONG. I love them for being my fans, I hate the smell they leave behind. I too can distance myself from my people. (*She looks around, then whispers in his ear.*) "Art for the masses" is a shitty excuse to keep artists poor. (*She pops a cigarette in her mouth.*) Be a gentleman, will you? And light my cigarette. (*Gallimard fumbles for a match.*)

GALLIMARD. I don't . . . smoke.

SONG. (*Lighting her own.*) Your loss. Had you lit my cigarette, I might have blown a puff of smoke right between your eyes. Come. (*They start to walk about the stage. It is a summer night on the Beijing streets. Sounds of the city play on the house speakers.*) How I wish there were even a tiny cafe to sit in. With cappuccinos, and men in tuxedos and bad expatriate jazz.

GALLIMARD. If my history serves me correctly, you weren't even allowed into the clubs in Shanghai before the Revolution.

SONG. Your history serves you poorly, Monsieur Gallimard. True, there were signs reading "No dogs and Chinamen." But a woman, especially a delicate Oriental woman — we always go where we please. Could you imagine it otherwise? Clubs in China filled with pasty, big-thighed white women, while thousands of slender lotus blossoms wait just outside the door? Never. The clubs would be empty. (*Beat.*) We have always held a certain fascination for you Caucasian men, have we not?

GALLIMARD. But . . . that fascination is imperialist, or so you tell me.

SONG. Do you believe everything I tell you? Yes. It is always imperialist. But sometimes . . . sometimes, it is also mutual. Oh — this is my flat.

GALLIMARD. I didn't even —

SONG. Thank you. Come another time and we will further expand your mind. (*Song exits. Gallimard continues roaming the streets as he speaks to us.*)

GALLIMARD. What was that? What did she mean, "Sometimes . . . it is mutual"? Women do not flirt with me. And I normally can't talk to them. But tonight, I held up my end of the conversation.

SCENE 9

Gallimard's bedroom. Beijing. 1960.
  Helga Enters.

HELGA. You didn't tell me you'd be home late.

GALLIMARD. I didn't intend to. Something came up.

HELGA. Oh? Like what?

GALLIMARD. I went to the . . . to the Dutch ambassador's home.

HELGA. Again?

GALLIMARD. There was a reception for a visiting scholar. He's writing a six-volume treatise on the Chinese revolution. We all gathered that meant he'd have to live here long enough to actually write six volumes, and we all expressed our deepest sympathies.

HELGA. Well, I had a good night too. I went with the ladies to a martial arts demonstration. Some of those men — when they break those thick boards — (*She mimes fanning herself.*) whoo-whoo! (*Helga exits. Lights dim.*)

22

GALLIMARD. I lied to my wife. Why? I've never had any reason to lie before. But what reason did I have tonight? I didn't do anything wrong. That night, I had a dream. Other people, I've been told, have dreams where angels appear. Or dragons, or Sophia Loren in a towel. In my dream, Marc from school appeared. (*Marc enters, in a nightshirt and cap.*)

MARC. Rene! You met a girl! (*Gallimard and Marc stumble down the Beijing streets. Night sounds over the speakers.*)

GALLIMARD. It's not that amazing, thank you.

MARC. No! It's so monumental, I heard about it halfway around the world in my sleep!

GALLIMARD. I've met girls before, you know.

MARC. Name one. I've come across time and space to congratulate you. (*He hands Gallimard a bottle of wine.*)

GALLIMARD. Marc, this is expensive.

MARC. On those rare occasions when you become a formless spirit, why not steal the best? (*Marc pops open the bottle, begins to share it with Gallimard.*)

GALLIMARD. You embarrass me. She . . . there's no reason to think she likes me.

MARC. "Sometimes, it is mutual"?

GALLIMARD. Oh.

MARC. "Mutual"? "Mutual"? What does that mean?

GALLIMARD. You heard?

MARC. It means the money is in the bank, you only have to write the check!

GALLIMARD. I am a married man!

MARC. And an excellent one too. I cheated after . . . six months. Then again and again, until now — three hundred girls in twelve years.

GALLIMARD. I don't think we should hold that up as a model.

MARC. Of course not! My life — it is disgusting! Phooey! Phooey! But, you — you are the model husband.

GALLIMARD. Anyway, it's impossible. I'm a foreigner.

MARC. Ah, yes. She cannot love you, it is taboo, but something deep inside her heart . . . she cannot help herself . . . she must surrender to you. It is her destiny.

GALLIMARD. How do you imagine all this?

MARC. The same way you do. It's an old story. It's in our

blood. They fear us, Rene. Their women fear us. And their men — their men hate us. And, you know something? They are all correct. (*They spot a light in a window.*) There! There, Rene!

GALLIMARD. It's her window.

MARC. Late at night — it burns. The light — it burns for you.

GALLIMARD. I won't look. It's not respectful.

MARC. We don't have to be respectful. We're foreign devils. (*Enter Song, in a sheer robe. The "One Fine Day" aria creeps in over the speakers. With her back to us, Song mimes attending to her toilette. Her robe comes loose, revealing her white shoulders.*) All your life you've waited for a beautiful girl who would lay down for you. All your life you've smiled like a saint when it's happened to every other man you know. And you see them in magazines and you see them in movies. And you wonder, what's wrong with me? Will anyone beautiful ever want me? As the years pass, your hair thins and you struggle to hold onto even your hopes. Stop struggling, Rene. The wait in over. (*He exits.*)

GALLIMARD. Marc? Marc? (*At that moment, Song, her back still towards us, drops her robe. A second of her naked back, then a sound cue: a phone ringing, very loud. Blackout, followed in the next beat by a special up on the bedroom area, where a phone now sits. Gallimard stumbles across the stage and picks up the phone. Sound cue out. Over the course of his conversation, area lights fill in the vicinity of his bed. It is the following morning.*) Yes? Hello?

SONG. (*Offstage.*) Is it very early?

GALLIMARD. Why, yes.

SONG. (*Offstage.*) How early?

GALLIMARD. It's . . . it's 5:30. Why are you — ?

SONG. (*Offstage.*) But it's light outside. Already.

GALLIMARD. It is. The sun must be in confusion today. (*Over the course of Song's next speech, her upstage special comes up again. She sits in a chair, legs crossed, in a robe, telephone to her ear.*)

SONG. I waited until I saw the sun. That was as much discipline as I could manage for one night. Do you forgive me?

GALLIMARD. Of course . . . for what?

SONG. Then I'll ask you quickly. Are you really interested in the opera?

GALLIMARD. Why, yes. Yes I am.

SONG. Then come again next Thursday. I am playing *The Drunken Beauty*. May I count on you?

GALLIMARD. Yes. You may.

SONG. Perfect. Well, I must be getting to bed. I'm exhausted. It's been a very long night for me. (*Song hangs up; special on her goes off. Gallimard begins to dress for work.*)

Scene 10

Song Liling's apartment. Beijing. 1960

GALLIMARD. I returned to the opera that next week, and the week after that . . . she keeps our meetings so short — perhaps fifteen, twenty minutes at most. So I am left each week with a thirst which is intensified. In this way, fifteen weeks have gone by. I am starting to doubt the words of my friend Marc. But no, not really. In my heart, I know she has . . . an interest in me. I suspect this is her way. She is outwardly bold and outspoken, yet her heart is shy and afraid. It is the Oriental in her at war with her Western education.

SONG. (*Offstage.*) I will be out in an instant. Ask the servant for anything you want.

GALLIMARD. Tonight, I have finally been invited to enter her apartment. Though the idea is almost beyond belief, I believe she is afraid of me. (*Gallimard looks around the room. He picks up a picture in a frame, studies it. Without his noticing, Song Enters, dressed elegantly in a black gown from the twenties. She stands in the doorway looking like Anna May Wong.*)

SONG. That is my father.

GALLIMARD. (*Surprised.*) Mademoiselle Song . . . (*She glides up to him, snatches away the picture.*)

SONG. It is very good that he did not live to see the Revolution. They would, no doubt, have made him kneel on broken glass. Not that he didn't deserve such a punishment. But he is my father. I would've hated to see it happen.

GALLIMARD. I'm very honored that you've allowed me to visit your home. (*Song curtseys.*)

SONG. Thank you. Oh! Haven't you been poured any tea?

GALLIMARD. I'm really not—

SONG. (*To her offstage servant.*) Shu-Fang! Cha! Kwai-lah! (*to Gallimard*) I'm sorry. You want everything to be perfect—

GALLIMARD. Please.

SONG. —and before the evening even begins—

GALLIMARD. I'm really not thirsty.

SONG. —it's ruined.

GALLIMARD. (*Sharply.*) Mademoiselle Song! (*Song sits down.*)

SONG. I'm sorry.

GALLIMARD. What are you apologizing for now? (*Pause; Song starts to giggle.*)

SONG. I don't know! (*Gallimard laughs.*)

GALLIMARD. Exactly my point.

SONG. Oh, I am silly. Lightheaded. I promise not to apologize for anything else tonight, do you hear me?

GALLIMARD. That's a good girl. (*Shu-Fang, a servant girl, comes out with a tea tray and starts to pour.*)

SONG. (*To Shu-Fang.*) No! I'll pour myself for the gentleman! (*Shu-Fang, staring at Gallimard, exits.*)

GALLIMARD. You have a beautiful home.

SONG. No, I . . . I don't even know why I invited you up.

GALLIMARD. Well, I'm glad you did. (*Song looks around the room.*)

SONG. There is an element of danger to your presence.

GALLIMARD. Oh?

SONG. You must know.

GALLIMARD. It doesn't concern me. We both know why I'm here.

SONG. It doesn't concern me either. No...well perhaps...

GALLIMARD. What?

SONG. Perhaps I am slightly afraid of scandal.

GALLIMARD. What are we doing?

SONG. I'm entertaining you. In my parlor.

26

GALLIMARD. In France, that would hardly —
SONG. France. France is a country living in the modern era. Perhaps even ahead of it. China is a nation whose soul is firmly rooted two thousand years in the past. What I do, even pouring the tea for you now . . . it has . . . implications. The walls and windows say so. Even my own heart, strapped inside this Western dress . . . even it says things — things I don't care to hear. (*Song hands Gallimard a cup of tea. Gallimard puts his hand over both the teacup and Song's hand.*)
GALLIMARD. This is a beautiful dress.
SONG. Don't.
GALLIMARD. What?
SONG. I don't even know if it looks right on me.
GALLIMARD. Believe me —
SONG. You are from France. You see so many beautiful women.
GALLIMARD. France? Since when are the European women — ?
SONG. Oh! What am I trying to do, anyway?! (*Song runs to the door, composes herself, then turns towards Gallimard.*) Monsieur Gallimard, perhaps you should go.
GALLIMARD. But . . . why?
SONG. There's something wrong about this.
GALLIMARD. I don't see what.
SONG. I feel . . . I am not myself.
GALLIMARD. No. You're nervous.
SONG. Please. Hard as I try to be modern, to speak like a man, to hold a Western woman's strong face up to my own . . . in the end, I fail. A small, frightened heart beats too quickly and gives me away. Monsieur Gallimard, I'm a Chinese girl. I've never . . . never invited a man up to my flat before. The forwardness of my actions makes my skin burn.
GALLIMARD. What are you afraid of? Certainly not me, I hope.
SONG. I'm a modest girl.
GALLIMARD. I know. And very beautiful (*He touches her hair.*)
SONG. Please — go now. The next time you see me, I shall again be myself.

GALLIMARD. I like you the way you are right now.

SONG. You are a cad.

GALLIMARD. What do you expect? I'm a foreign devil. (*Gallimard walks* D.S. *Song exits. To us.*) Did you hear the way she talked about Western women? Much differently than the first night. She does — she feels inferior to them — and to me.

Scene 11

The French embassy. Beijing. 1960.
Gallimard moves towards a desk.

GALLIMARD. I determined to try an experiment. In *Madame Butterfly*, Cio-Cio-San fears that the Western man who catches a butterfly will pierce its heart with a needle, then leave it to perish. I began to wonder: had I too, caught a butterfly who would writhe on a needle? (*Marc enters, dressed as a bureaucrat, holding a stack of papers. As Gallimard speaks, Marc hands papers to him. He peruses, then signs, stamps or rejects them.*) Over the next five weeks, I worked like a dynamo. I stopped going to the opera, I didn't phone or write her. I knew this little flower was waiting for me to call, and, as I wickedly refused to do so, I felt for the first time that rush of power — the absolute power of a man. (*Marc continues acting as the bureaucrat, but he now speaks as himself.*)

MARC. Rene! It's me!

GALLIMARD. Marc — I hear your voice everywhere now. Even in the midst of work.

MARC. That's because I'm watching you — all the time.

GALLIMARD. You were always the most popular guy in school.

MARC. Well, there's no guarantee of failure in life like happiness in high school. Somehow I knew I'd end up in the suburbs working for Renault and you'd be in the Orient picking exotic women off the trees. And they say there's no justice.

GALLIMARD. That's why you were my friend?

28

MARC. I gave you a little of my life, so that now you can give me some of yours. (*Pause.*) Remember Isabelle?

GALLIMARD. Of course I remember! She was my first experience.

MARC. We all wanted to ball her. But she only wanted me.

GALLIMARD. I had her.

MARC. Right. You balled her.

GALLIMARD. You were the only one who ever believed me.

MARC. Well, there's a good reason for that. (*Beat.*) C'mon. You must've guessed.

GALLIMARD. You told me to wait in the bushes by the cafeteria that night. The next thing I knew, she was on me. Dress up in the air.

MARC. She never wore underwear.

GALLIMARD. My arms were pinned to the dirt.

MARC. She loved the superior position. A girl ahead of her time.

GALLIMARD. I looked up, and there was this woman . . . bouncing up and down on my loins.

MARC. Screaming, right?

GALLIMARD. Screaming, and breaking off the branches all around me, and pounding my butt up and down into the dirt.

MARC. Huffing and puffing like a locomotive.

GALLIMARD. And in the middle of all this, the leaves were getting into my mouth, my legs were losing circulation, I thought, "God. So this is *it*?"

MARC. You thought that?

GALLIMARD. Well, I was worried about my legs falling off.

MARC. You didn't have a good time?

GALLIMARD. No, that's not what I — I had a great time!

MARC. You're sure?

GALLIMARD. Yeah. Really.

MARC. 'Cuz I wanted you to have a good time.

GALLIMARD. I did. (*Pause.*)

MARC. Shit. (*Pause.*) When all is said and done, she was kind of a lousy lay, wasn't she? I mean, there was a lot of energy there, but you never knew what she was doing with it. Like when she yelled "I'm coming!" — hell, it was so loud, you wanted to go "Look, it's not that big a deal."

GALLIMARD. I got scared. I thought she meant someone was actually coming. (*Pause.*) But, Marc?

MARC. What?

GALLIMARD. Thanks.

MARC. Oh, don't mention it.

GALLIMARD. It was my first experience.

MARC. Yeah. You got her.

GALLIMARD. I got her.

MARC. Wait! Look at that letter again! (*Gallimard picks up one of the papers he's been stamping, and rereads it.*)

GALLIMARD. (*To us.*) After six weeks, they began to arrive. The letters. (*Upstage special on Song, as Madame Butterfly. The scene is underscored by the "Love Duet."*)

SONG. Did we fight? I do not know. Is the opera no longer of interest to you? Please come — my audiences miss the white devil in their midst. (*Gallimard looks up from the letter, towards us.*)

GALLIMARD. (*To us.*) A concession, but much too dignified. (*Beat; he discards the letter.*) I skipped the opera again that week to complete a position paper on trade. (*The bureaucrat hands him another letter.*)

SONG. Six weeks have passed since last we met. Is this your practice — to leave friends in the lurch? Sometimes I hate you, sometimes I hate myself, but always I miss you.

GALLIMARD. (*To us.*) Better, but I don't like the way she calls me "friend." When a woman calls a man her "friend," she's calling him a eunuch or a homosexual. (*Beat; he discards the letter.*) I was absent from the opera for the seventh week, feeling a sudden urge to clean out my files. (*Bureaucrat hands him another letter.*)

SONG. Your rudeness is beyond belief. I don't deserve this cruelty. Don't bother to call. I'll have you turned away at the door.

GALLIMARD. (*To us.*) I didn't. (*He discards the letter; bureaucrat hands him another.*) And then finally, the letter that concluded my experiment.

SONG. I am out of words, I can hide behind dignity no longer. What do you want? I have already given you my

30

shame. (*Gallimard gives the letter back to Marc, slowly. Special on Song fades out.*)

GALLIMARD. (*To us.*) Reading it, I became suddenly ashamed. Yes, my experiment had been a success. She was turning on my needle. But the victory seemed hollow.

MARC. Hollow?! Are you crazy?

GALLIMARD. Nothing, Marc. Please go away.

MARC. (*Exiting, with papers.*) Haven't I taught you anything?

GALLIMARD. "I have already given you my shame." I had to attend a reception that evening. On the way, I felt sick. If there is a God, surely he would punish me now. I had finally gained power over a beautiful woman, only to abuse it cruelly. There must be justice in the world. I had the strange feeling that the ax would fall this very evening.

SCENE 12

Ambassador Toulon's residence. Beijing. 1960.
Sound cue: party noises. Light change. We are now in a spacious residence. Toulon, the French ambassador, Enters and taps Gallimard on the shoulder.

TOULON. Gallimard? Can I have a word? Over here.

GALLIMARD. (*To us.*) Manuel Toulon. French ambassador to China. He likes to think of us all as his children. Rather like God.

TOULON. Look, Gallimard, there's not much to say. I've liked you. From the day you walked in. You were no leader, but you were tidy and efficient.

GALLIMARD. Thank you, sir.

TOULON. Don't jump the gun. Okay, our needs in China are changing. It's embarrassing that we lost Indochina. Someone just wasn't on the ball there. I don't mean you personally, of course.

GALLIMARD. Thank you, sir.

TOULON. We're going to be doing a lot more information-gathering in the future. The nature of our work here is changing. Some people are just going to have to go. It's nothing personal.

GALLIMARD. Oh.

TOULON. Want to know a secret? Vice-Consul LeBon is being transferred.

GALLIMARD. (*To us.*) My immediate superior!

TOULON. And most of his department.

GALLIMARD. (*To us.*) Just as I feared! God has seen my evil heart —

TOULON. But not you.

GALLIMARD. (*To us.*) — and he's taking her away just as . . . (*To Toulon.*) Excuse me, sir?

TOULON. Scare you? I think I did. Cheer up, Gallimard. I want you to replace LeBon as vice-consul.

GALLIMARD. You — ? Yes, well, thank you, sir.

TOULON. Anytime.

GALLIMARD. I . . . accept with great humility.

TOULON. Humility won't be part of the job. You're going to coordinate the revamped intelligence division. Want to know a secret? A year ago, you would've been out. But the past few months, I don't know how it happened, you've become this new aggressive confident . . . thing. And they also tell me you get along with the Chinese. So I think you're a lucky man, Gallimard. Congratulations. (*They shake hands. Toulon exits. Party noises out. Gallimard stumbles across a darkened stage.*)

GALLIMARD. Vice-consul? Impossible! As I stumbled out of the party, I saw it written across the sky: There is no God. Or, no — say that there is a God. But that God . . . understands. Of course! God who creates Eve to serve Adam, who blesses Solomon with his harem but ties Jezebel to a burning bed — that God is a man. And he understands! At age thirty-nine, I was suddenly initiated into the way of the world.

SCENE 13

Song Liling's apartment. Beijing. 1960.
Song Enters, in a sheer dressing gown.

SONG. Are you crazy?

GALLIMARD. Mademoiselle Song —

32

SONG. To come here — at this hour? After . . . after eight weeks?

GALLIMARD. It's the most amazing —

SONG. You bang on my door? Scare my servants, scandalize the neighbors?

GALLIMARD. I've been promoted. To vice-consul. (*Pause.*)

SONG. And what is that supposed to mean to me?

GALLIMARD. Are you my Butterfly?

SONG. What are you saying?

GALLIMARD. I've come tonight for an answer: are you my Butterfly?

SONG. Don't you know already?

GALLIMARD. I want you to say it.

SONG. I don't want to say it.

GALLIMARD. So, that is your answer?

SONG. You know how I feel about —

GALLIMARD. I do remember one thing.

SONG. What?

GALLIMARD. In the letter I received today.

SONG. Don't.

GALLIMARD. "I have already given you my shame."

SONG. It's enough that I even wrote it.

GALLIMARD. Well, then —

SONG. I shouldn't have it splashed across my face.

GALLIMARD. — if that's all true —

SONG. Stop!

GALLIMARD. Then what is one more short answer?

SONG. I don't want to!

GALLIMARD. Are you my Butterfly? (*Silence; he crosses the room and begins to touch her hair.*) I want from you honesty. There should be nothing false between us. No false pride. (*Pause.*)

SONG. Yes, I am. I am your Butterfly.

GALLIMARD. Then let me be honest with you. It is because of you that I was promoted tonight. You have changed my life forever. My little Butterfly, there should be no more secrets: I love you. (*He starts to kiss her roughly. She resists slightly.*)

SONG.   No . . . no . . . gently . . . please,   I've never . . .

GALLIMARD. No?

SONG. I've tried to appear experienced, but . . . the truth is . . . no.

GALLIMARD. Are you cold?

SONG. Yes. Cold.

GALLIMARD. Then we will go very, very slowly. (*He starts to caress her; her gown begins to open.*)

SONG. No . . . let me . . . keep my clothes . . .

GALLIMARD. But . . .

SONG. Please . . . it all frightens me. I'm a modest Chinese girl.

GALLIMARD. My poor little treasure.

SONG. I am your treasure. Though inexperienced, I am not . . . ignorant. They teach us things, our mothers, about pleasing a man.

GALLIMARD. Yes?

SONG. I'll do my best to make you happy. Turn off the lights. (*Gallimard gets up and heads for a lamp. Song, propped up on one elbow, tosses her hair back and smiles.*)

SONG. Monsieur Gallimard?

GALLIMARD. Yes, Butterfly?

SONG. "Vieni, vieni!"

GALLIMARD. "Come, darling."

SONG. "Ah! Dolce notte!"

GALLIMARD. "Beautiful night."

SONG. "Tutto estatico d'amor ride il ciel!"

GALLIMARD. "All ecstatic with love, the heavens are filled with laughter." (*He turns off the lamp. Blackout.*)

ACT TWO

Scene 1

M. Gallimard's cell. Paris, 1988.
Lights up on Gallimard. He sits in his cell, reading from a leaflet.

GALLIMARD. This, from a contemporary critic's commentary on *Madame Butterfly*: "Pinkerton suffers from . . . being an obnoxious bounder whom every man in the audience itches to kick." Bully for us men in the audience! Then, in the same note: "Butterfly is the most irresistibly appealing of Puccini's 'Little Women.' Watching the succession of her humiliations is like watching a child under torture." (*He tosses the pamphlet over his shoulder.*) I suggest that, while we men may all want to kick Pinkerton, very few of us would pass up the opportunity to be Pinkerton. (*Gallimard moves out of his cell.*)

Scene 2

Gallimard and Butterfly's flat. Beijing. 1960.
We are in a simple but well-decorated parlor. Gallimard moves to sit on a sofa, while Song, dressed in a chong sam, Enters and curls up at his feet.

GALLIMARD. (*To us.*) We secured a flat on the outskirts of Peking. Butterfly, as I was calling her now, decorated our "home" with Western furniture and Chinese antiques. And there, on a few stolen afternoons or evenings each week, Butterfly commenced her education.
SONG. The Chinese men — they keep us down.
GALLIMARD. Even in the "New Society"?
SONG. In the "New Society," we are all kept ignorant equally. That's one of the exciting things about loving a

35

Western man. I know you are not threatened by a woman's education.

GALLIMARD. I'm no saint, Butterfly.

SONG. But you come from a progressive society.

GALLIMARD. We're not always reminding each other how "old" we are, if that's what you mean.

SONG. Exactly. We Chinese — once, I suppose, it is true, we ruled the world. But so what? How much more exciting to be part of the society ruling the world today. Tell me — what's happening in Vietnam?

GALLIMARD. Oh, Butterfly — you want me to bring my work home?

SONG. I want to know what you know. To be impressed by my man. It's not the particulars so much as the fact that you're making decisions which change the shape of the world.

GALLIMARD. Not the world. At best, a small corner. (*Toulon enters.*)

SCENE 3

French embassy. Beijing. 1961.
    Gallimard moves D.S., *to Toulon. Song remains* U.S., *watching.*

TOULON. And a more troublesome corner is hard to imagine.

GALLIMARD. So, the Americans plan to begin bombing?

TOULON. This is very secret, Gallimard: yes. The Americans don't have an embassy here. They're asking us to be their eyes and ears. Say Jack Kennedy signed an order to bomb North Vietnam, Laos. How would the Chinese react?

GALLIMARD. I think the Chinese will squawk —

TOULON. Uh-huh.

GALLIMARD. — but, in their hearts, they don't even like Ho Chi Minh. (*Pause.*)

TOULON. What a bunch of jerks. Vietnam was *our* colony. Not only didn't the Americans help us fight to keep them, but now, seven years later, they've come back to grab the territory for themselves. It's very irritating.

GALLIMARD. With all due respect, sir, why should the Americans have won our war for us back in '54 if we didn't have the will to win it ourselves?

TOULON. You're kidding, aren't you? (*Pause.*)

GALLIMARD. The Orientals simply want to be associated with whoever shows the most strength and power. You live with the Chinese, sir. Do you think they like Communism?

TOULON. I live in China. Not with the Chinese.

GALLIMARD. Well, I —

TOULON. *You* live with the Chinese.

GALLIMARD. Excuse me?

TOULON. I can't keep a secret.

GALLIMARD. What are you saying?

TOULON. Only that I'm not immune to gossip. So, you're keeping a native mistress? Don't answer. It's none of my business. (*Pause.*) I'm sure she must be gorgeous.

GALLIMARD. Well . . .

TOULON. I'm impressed. You had the stamina to go out into the streets and hunt one down. Some of us have to be content with the wives of the expatriate community.

GALLIMARD. I do feel . . . fortunate.

TOULON. So, Gallimard, you've got the inside knowledge —what *do* the Chinese think?

GALLIMARD. Deep down, they miss the old days. You know, cappuccinos, men in tuxedos —

TOULON. So what do we tell the Americans about Vietnam?

GALLIMARD. Tell them there's a natural affinity between the West and the Orient.

TOULON. And that you speak from experience?

GALLIMARD. The Orientals are people too. They want the good things we can give them. If the Americans demonstrate the will to win, the Vietnamese will welcome them into a mutually beneficial union.

TOULON. I don't see how the Vietnamese can stand up to American firepower.

GALLIMARD. Orientals will always submit to a greater force.

37

TOULON. I'll note your opinions in my report. The Americans always love to hear how "welcome" they'll be. (*He starts to exit.*)

GALLIMARD. Sir?

TOULON. Mmmm?

GALLIMARD. This . . . rumor you've heard.

TOULON. Uh-huh?

GALLIMARD. How . . . widespread do you think it is?

TOULON. It's only widespread within this embassy. Where nobody talks because everybody is guilty. We were worried about you, Gallimard. We thought you were the only one here without a secret. Now you go and find a lotus blossom . . . and top us all. (*He exits.*)

GALLIMARD. (*To us.*) Toulon knows! And he approves! I was learning the benefits of being a man. We form our own clubs, sit behind thick doors, smoke — and celebrate the fact that we're still boys. (*He starts to move* U.S., *towards Song.*) So, over the — (*Suddenly Comrade Chin Enters. Gallimard backs away. To Song.*) No! Why does she have to come in?

SONG. Rene, be sensible. How can they understand the story without her? Now, don't embarrass yourself. (*Gallimard moves* D.C.)

GALLIMARD. (*To us.*) Now, you will see why my story is so amusing to so many people. Why they snicker at parties in disbelief. Please — try to understand it from my point of view. We are all prisoners of our time and place. (*He exits.*)

SCENE 4

Gallimard and Butterfly's flat. Beijing. 1961.

SONG. (*To us.*) 1961. The flat Monsieur Gallimard rented for us. An evening after he has gone.

CHIN. Okay, see if you can find out when the Americans plan to start bombing Vietnam. If you can find out what cities, even better.

SONG. I'll do my best, but I don't want to arouse his suspicions.

CHIN. Yeah, sure, of course. So, what else?

SONG. The Americans will increase troops in Vietnam to 170,000 soldiers with 120,000 militia and 11,000 American advisors.

CHIN. (*Writing.*) Wait, wait, 120,000 militia and—

SONG. —11,000 American—

CHIN. —American advisors. (*Beat.*) How do you remember so much?

SONG. I'm an actor.

CHIN. Yeah. (*Beat.*) Is that how come you dress like that?

SONG. Like what, Miss Chin?

CHIN. Like that dress! You're wearing a dress. And every time I come here, you're wearing a dress. Is that because you're an actor? Or what?

SONG. It's a . . . disguise, Miss Chin.

CHIN. Actors, I think they're all weirdos. My mother tells me actors are like gamblers or prostitutes or—

SONG. It helps me in my assignment. (*Pause.*)

CHIN. You're not gathering information in any way that violates Communist Party principles, are you?

SONG. Why would I do that?

CHIN. Just checking. Remember: when working for the Great Proletarian State, you represent our Chairman Mao in every position you take.

SONG. I'll try to imagine the Chairman taking my positions.

CHIN. We all think of him this way. Good-bye, comrade. (*She starts to exit.*) Comrade?

SONG. Yes?

CHIN. Don't forget: there is no homosexuality in China!

SONG. Yes, I've heard.

CHIN. Just checking. (*She exits.*)

SONG. (*To us.*) What passes for a woman in modern China. (*Gallimard sticks his head out from the wings.*)

GALLIMARD. Is she gone?

SONG. Yes, Rene. Please continue in your own fashion.

SCENE 5

Beijing. 1961–63.
    Gallimard moves to the couch where Song still sits. He lies down in her lap, and she strokes his forehead.

39

GALLIMARD. (*To us.*) And so, over the years, 1961, '62, '63, we settled into our routine, Butterfly and I. She would always have prepared a light snack and then, ever so delicately, and only if I agreed, she would start to pleasure me. With her hands, her mouth . . . too many ways to explain, and too sad, given my present situation. But mostly we would talk. About my life. Perhaps there is nothing more rare than to find a woman who passionately listens. (*Song remains* U.S., *listening, as Helga enters and plays a scene* D.S. *with Gallimard.*)

HELGA. Rene, I visited Dr. Bolleart this morning.

GALLIMARD. Why? Are you ill?

HELGA. No, no. You see, I wanted to ask him . . . that question we've been discussing.

GALLIMARD. And I told you, it's only a matter of time. Why did you bring a doctor into this? We just have to keep trying — like a crapshoot, actually.

HELGA. I went, I'm sorry. But listen: he says there's nothing wrong with me.

GALLIMARD. You see? Now, will you stop — ?

HELGA. Rene, he says he'd like you to go in and take some tests.

GALLIMARD. Why? So he can find there's nothing wrong with both of us?

HELGA. Rene, I don't ask for much. One trip! One visit! And then, whatever you want to do about it — you decide.

GALLIMARD. You're assuming he'll find something defective!

HELGA. No! Of course not! Whatever he finds — if he finds nothing, we decide what to do about nothing! But go!

GALLIMARD. If he finds nothing, we keep trying. Just like we do now.

HELGA. But at least we'll know! (*Pause.*) I'm sorry. (*She starts to exit.*)

GALLIMARD. Do you really want me to see Dr. Bolleart?

HELGA. Only if you want a child, Rene. We have to face the fact that time is running out. Only if you want a child. (*She exits.*)

GALLIMARD. (*To Song.*) I'm a modern man, Butterfly. And yet, I don't want to go. It's the same old voodoo. I feel like God himself is laughing at me if I can't produce a child.

SONG. You men of the West — you're obsessed by your odd desire for equality. Your wife can't give you a child, and *you're* going to the doctor?
GALLIMARD. Well, you see, she's already gone.
SONG. And because this incompetent can't find the defect, you now have to subject yourself to him? It's unnatural.
GALLIMARD. Well, what is the "natural" solution?
SONG. In Imperial China, when a man found that one wife was inadequate, he turned to another — to give him his son.
GALLIMARD. What do you —? I can't . . . marry you, yet.
SONG. Please. I'm not asking you to be my husband. But I am already your wife.
GALLIMARD. Do you want to . . . have my child?
SONG. I thought you'd never ask.
GALLIMARD. But, your career . . . your —
SONG. Phooey on my career! That's your Western mind, twisting itself into strange shapes again. Of course I love my career. But what would I love most of all? To feel something inside me — day and night — something I know is yours. (*Pause.*) Promise me . . . you won't go to this doctor. Who is this Western quack to set himself as judge over the man I love? I know who is a man, and who is not. (*She exits.*)
GALLIMARD. (*To us.*) Dr. Bolleart? Of course I didn't go. What man would?

SCENE 6

Beijing. 1963.
   Party noises over the house speakers. Renee Enters, wearing a revealing gown.

GALLIMARD. 1963. A party at the Austrian embassy. None of us could remember the Austrian ambassador's name, which seemed somehow appropriate. (*To Renee.*) So, I tell the Americans, Diem must go. The U.S. wants to be respected by the Vietnamese, and yet they're propping up this nobody seminarian as her president. A man whose claim to fame is his sister-in-law imposing fanatic "moral order"

41

campaigns? Oriental women — when they're good, they're very good, but when they're bad, they're Christians.

RENEE. Yeah.

GALLIMARD. And what do you do?

RENEE. I'm a student. My father exports a lot of useless stuff to the Third World.

GALLIMARD. How useless?

RENEE. You know. Squirt guns, confectioner's sugar, hula hoops . . .

GALLIMARD. I'm sure they appreciate the sugar.

RENEE. I'm here for two years to study Chinese.

GALLIMARD. Two years!

RENEE. That's what everybody says.

GALLIMARD. When did you arrive?

RENEE. Three weeks ago.

GALLIMARD. And?

RENEE. I like it. It's primitive, but . . . well, this is the place to learn Chinese, so here I am.

GALLIMARD. Why Chinese?

RENEE. I think it'll be important someday.

GALLIMARD. You do?

RENEE. Don't ask me when, but . . . that's what I think.

GALLIMARD. Well, I agree with you. One hundred percent. That's very farsighted.

RENEE. Yeah. Well of course, my father thinks I'm a complete weirdo.

GALLIMARD. He'll thank you someday.

RENEE. Like when the Chinese start buying hula hoops?

GALLIMARD. There're a billion bellies out there.

RENEE. And if they end up taking over the world — well, then I'll be lucky to know Chinese too, right? (*Pause.*)

GALLIMARD. At this point, I don't see how the Chinese can possibly take —

RENEE. You know what I *don't* like about China?

GALLIMARD. Excuse me? No — what?

RENEE. Nothing to do at night.

GALLIMARD. You come to parties at embassies like everyone else.

RENEE. Yeah, but they get out at ten. And then what?

GALLIMARD. I'm afraid the Chinese idea of a dance hall is

42

a dirt floor and a man with a flute.

RENEE. Are you married?

GALLIMARD. Yes. Why?

RENEE. You wanna . . . fool around? (*Pause.*)

GALLIMARD. Sure.

RENEE. I'll wait for you outside. What's your name?

GALLIMARD. Gallimard. Rene.

RENEE. Weird. I'm Renee too. (*She exits.*)

GALLIMARD. (*To us.*) And so, I embarked on my first extra-extramarital affair. Renee was picture perfect. With a body like those girls in the magazines. If I put a tissue paper over my eyes, I wouldn't have been able to tell the difference. And it was exciting to be with someone who wasn't afraid to be seen completely naked. But is it possible for a woman to be *too* uninhibited, *too* willing, so as to seem almost too . . . masculine? (*Chuck Berry blares from the house speakers, then comes down in volume as Renee Enters, toweling her hair.*)

RENEE. You have a nice weenie.

GALLIMARD. What?

RENEE. Penis. You have a nice penis.

GALLIMARD. Oh. Well, thank you. That's very . . .

RENEE. What — can't take a compliment?

GALLIMARD. No, it's very . . . reassuring.

RENEE. But most girls don't come out and say it, huh?

GALLIMARD. And also . . . what did you call it?

RENEE. Oh. Most girls don't call it a "weenie," huh?

GALLIMARD. It sounds very —

RENEE. Small, I know.

GALLIMARD. I was going to say, "young."

RENEE. Yeah. Young, small, same thing. Most guys are pretty, uh, sensitive about that. Like, you know, I had a boyfriend back home in Denmark. I got mad at him once and called him a little weeniehead. He got so mad! He said at least I should call him a great big weeniehead.

GALLIMARD. I suppose I just say "penis."

RENEE. Yeah. That's pretty clinical. There's "cock," but that sounds like a chicken. And "prick" is painful, and "dick" is like you're talking about someone who's not in the room.

43

GALLIMARD. Yes. It's a . . . bigger problem than I imagined.

RENEE. I — I think maybe it's because I really don't know what to do with them — that's why I call them "weenies."

GALLIMARD. Well, you did quite well with . . . mine.

RENEE. Thanks, but I mean, really *do* with them. Like, okay, have you ever looked at one? I mean, really?

GALLIMARD. No, I suppose when it's part of you, you sort of take it for granted.

RENEE. I guess. But, like, it just hangs there. This little . . . flap of flesh. And there's so much fuss that we make about it. Like, I think the reason we fight wars is because we wear clothes. Because no one knows — between the men, I mean — who has the biggest . . . weenie. So, if I'm a guy with a small one, I'm going to build a really big building or take over a really big piece of land or write a really long book so the other men don't know, right? But, see, it never really works, that's the problem. I mean, you conquer the country, or whatever, but you're still wearing clothes, so there's no way to prove absolutely whose is bigger or smaller. And that's what we call a civilized society. The whole world run by a bunch of men with pricks the size of pins. (*She exits.*)

GALLIMARD. (*To us.*) This was simply not acceptable. (*A high-pitched chime rings through the air. Song, dressed as Butterfly, appears in the u.s. special. She is obviously distressed. Her body swoons as she attempts to clip the stems of flowers she's arranging in a vase.*) But I kept up our affair, wildly, for several months. Why? I believe because of Butterfly. She knew the secret I was trying to hide. But, unlike a Western woman, she didn't confront me, threaten, even pout. I remembered the words of Puccini's *Butterfly*:

SONG. "Noi siamo gente avvezze/ alle piccole cose/ umili e silenziose."

GALLIMARD. "I come from a people/ Who are accustomed to little/ Humble and silent." I saw Pinkerton and Butterfly, and what she would say if he were unfaithful . . . nothing. She would cry, alone, into those wildly soft sleeves, once full of possessions, now empty to collect her tears. It was her tears and her silence that excited me, every time I visited Renee.

TOULON. (*Offstage.*) Gallimard! (*Toulon enters. Gallimard turns towards him. During the next section, Song, U.S., begins to dance with the flowers. It is a drunken, reckless dance, where she breaks small pieces off the stems.*) They're killing him.

GALLIMARD. Who? I'm sorry? What?

TOULON. Bother you to come over at this late hour?

GALLIMARD. No . . . of course not.

TOULON. Not after you hear my secret. Champagne?

GALLIMARD. Um . . . thank you.

TOULON. You're surprised. There's something that you've wanted, Gallimard. No, not a promotion. Next time. Something in the world. You're not aware of this, but there's an informal gossip circle among intelligence agents. And some of ours heard from some of the Americans—

GALLIMARD. Yes?

TOULON. That the U.S. will allow the Vietnamese generals to stage a coup . . . and assassinate President Diem. (*The chime rings again. Toulon freezes. Gallimard turns U.S. and looks at Butterfly, who slowly and deliberately clips a flower off its stem. Gallimard turns back towards Toulon.*)

GALLIMARD. I think . . . that's a very wise move! (*Toulon unfreezes.*)

TOULON. It's what you've been advocating. A toast?

GALLIMARD. Sure. I consider this a vindication.

TOULON. Not exactly. "To the test. Let's hope you pass." (*They drink. The chime rings again. Toulon freezes. Gallimard turns U.S., and Song clips another flower.*)

GALLIMARD. (*To Toulon.*) The test?

TOULON. (*Unfreezing.*) It's a test of everything you've been saying. I personally think the generals probably will stop the Communists. And you'll be a hero. But if anything goes wrong, then your opinions won't be worth a pig's ear. I'm sure that won't happen. But sometimes it's easier when they don't listen to you.

GALLIMARD. They're your opinions too, aren't they?

TOULON. Personally, yes.

GALLIMARD. So we agree.

TOULON. But my opinions aren't on that report. Yours are. Cheers. (*Toulon turns away from Gallimard and raises his glass. At that instant Song picks up the vase and hurls it to the*

45

ground. It shatters. Song sinks down amidst the shards of the vase, in a calm, childlike trance. She sings softly, as if reciting a child's nursery rhyme.)

SONG. (*Repeat as necessary.*) "The whole world over, the white man travels, setting anchor, wherever he likes. Life's not worth living, unless he finds, the finest maidens, of every land . . . " (*Gallimard turns* D.S. *towards us. Song continues singing.*)

GALLIMARD. I shook as I left his house. That coward! That worm! To put the burden for his decisions on my shoulders!

I started for Renee's. But no, that was all I needed. A schoolgirl who would question the role of the penis in modern society. What I wanted was revenge. A vessel to contain my humiliation. Though I hadn't seen her in several weeks, I headed for Butterfly's. (*Gallimard enters Song's apartment.*)

SONG. Oh! Rene . . . I was dreaming!

GALLIMARD. You've been drinking?

SONG. If I can't sleep, then yes, I drink. But then, it gives me these dreams which — Rene, it's been almost three weeks since you visited me last.

GALLIMARD. I know. There's been a lot going on in the world.

SONG. Fortunately I am drunk. So I can speak freely. It's not the world, it's you and me. And an old problem. Even the softest skin becomes like leather to a man who's touched it too often. I confess I don't know how to stop it. I don't know how to become another woman.

GALLIMARD. I have a request.

SONG. Is this a solution? Or are you ready to give up the flat?

GALLIMARD. It may be a solution. But I'm sure you won't like it.

SONG. Oh well, that's very important. "Like it?" Do you think I "like" lying here alone, waiting, always waiting for your return? Please — don't worry about what I may not "like."

GALLIMARD. I want to see you . . . naked. (*Silence.*)

SONG. I thought you understood my modesty. So you want

46

me to — what — strip? Like a big cowboy girl? Shiny pasties on my breasts? Shall I fling my kimono over my head and yell "ya-hoo" in the process? I thought you respected my shame!

GALLIMARD. I believe you gave me your shame many years ago.

SONG. Yes — and it is just like a white devil to use it against me. I can't believe it. I thought myself so repulsed by the passive Oriental and the cruel white man. Now I see — we are always most revolted by the things hidden within us.

GALLIMARD. I just mean —

SONG. Yes?

GALLIMARD. —that it will remove the only barrier left between us.

SONG. No, Rene. Don't couch your request in sweet words. Be yourself — a cad — and know that my love is enough, that I submit — submit to the worst you can give me. (*Pause.*) Well, come. Strip me. Whatever happens, know that you have willed it. Our love, in your hands. I'm helpless before my man. (*Gallimard starts to cross the room.*)

GALLIMARD. (*To us.*) Did I not undress her because I knew, somewhere deep down, what I would find? Perhaps. Happiness is so rare that our mind can turn somersaults to protect it.

At the time, I only knew that I was seeing Pinkerton stalking towards his Butterfly, ready to reward her love with his lecherous hands. The image sickened me, pulled me to my knees, so I was crawling towards her like a worm. By the time I reached her, Pinkerton . . . had vanished from my heart. To be replaced by something new, something unnatural, that flew in the face of all I'd learned in the world — something very close to love. (*He grabs her around the waist; she strokes his hair.*) Butterfly, forgive me.

SONG. Rene . . .

GALLIMARD. For everything. From the start.

Song. I'm . . .

GALLIMARD. I want to —

SONG. I'm pregnant. (*Beat.*) I'm pregnant. (*Beat.*) I'm pregnant. (*Beat.*)

GALLIMARD. I want to marry you!

47

SCENE 7

Gallimard and Butterfly's flat. Beijing. 1963.
    Downstage, Song paces as Comrade Chin reads from her notepad. Upstage, Gallimard is still kneeling. He remains on his knees throughout the scene, watching it.

SONG. I need a baby.
CHIN. (*From pad.*) He's been spotted going to a dorm.
SONG. I need a baby.
CHIN. At the Foreign Language Institute.
SONG. I need a baby.
CHIN. The room of a Danish girl . . . What do you mean, you need a baby?!
SONG. Tell Comrade Kang — last night, the entire mission, it could've ended.
CHIN. What do you mean?
SONG. Tell Kang — he told me to strip.
CHIN. Strip?!
SONG. Write!
CHIN. I tell you, I don't understand nothing about this case anymore. Nothing.
SONG. He told me to strip, and I took a chance. Oh, we Chinese, we know how to gamble.
CHIN. (*Writing.*) ". . . told him to strip."
SONG. My palms were wet, I had to make a split-second decision.
CHIN. Hey! Can you slow down?! (*Pause.*)
SONG. You write faster, I'm the artist here. Suddenly, it hit me — "All he wants is for her to submit. Once a woman submits, a man is always ready to become 'generous.'"
CHIN. You're just gonna end up with rough notes.
SONG. And it worked! He gave in! Now, if I can just present him with a baby. A Chinese baby with blond hair — he'll be mine for life!
CHIN. Kang will never agree! The trading of babies has to be a counterrevolutionary act!
SONG. Sometimes, a counterrevolutionary act is necessary to counter a counterrevolutionary act. (*Pause.*)

48

CHIN. Wait.

SONG. I need one . . . in seven months. Make sure it's a boy.

CHIN. This doesn't sound like something the Chairman would do. Maybe you'd better talk to Comrade Kang yourself.

SONG. Good. I will. (*Chin gets up to leave.*) Miss Chin? Why, in the Peking Opera, are women's roles played by men?

CHIN. I don't know. Maybe, a reactionary remnant of male —

SONG. No. (*Beat.*) Because only a man knows how a woman is supposed to act. (*Chin exits. Song turns* U.S., *towards Gallimard.*)

GALLIMARD. (*Calling after Chin.*) Good riddance! (*To song.*)

I could forget all that betrayal in an instant, you know. If you'd just come back and become Butterfly again.

SONG. Fat chance. You're here in prison, rotting in a cell. And I'm on a plane, winging my way back to China. Your President pardoned me of our treason, you know.

GALLIMARD. Yes, I read about that.

SONG. Must make you feel . . . lower than shit.

GALLIMARD. But don't you, even a little bit, wish you were here with me?

SONG. I'm an artist, Rene. You were my greatest . . . acting challenge. (*She laughs.*) It doesn't matter how rotten I answer, does it? You still adore me. That's why I love you, Rene. (*She points to us.*) So — you were telling your audience about the night I announced I was pregnant. (*Gallimard puts his arms around Song's waist. He and Song are in the positions they were in at the end of Scene 6.*)

SCENE 8

Same.

GALLIMARD. I'll divorce my wife. We'll live together here, and then later in France.

SONG. I feel so . . . ashamed.

49

GALLIMARD. Why?

SONG. I had begun to lose faith. And now, you shame me with your generosity.

GALLIMARD. Generosity? No, I'm proposing for very self-ish reasons.

SONG. Your apologies only make me feel more ashamed. My outburst a moment ago!

GALLIMARD. Your outburst? What about my request?!

SONG. You've been very patient dealing with my . . . ec-centricities. A Western man, used to women freer with their bodies —

GALLIMARD. It was sick! Don't make excuses for me.

SONG. I have to. You don't seem willing to make them for yourself. (*Pause.*)

GALLIMARD. You're crazy.

SONG. I'm happy. Which often looks like crazy.

GALLIMARD. Then make me crazy. Marry me. (*Pause.*)

SONG. No.

GALLIMARD. What?

SONG. Do I sound silly, a slave, if I say I'm not worthy?

GALLIMARD. Yes. In fact you do. No one has loved me like you.

SONG. Thank you. And no one ever will. I'll see to that.

GALLIMARD. So what is the problem?

SONG. Rene, we Chinese are realists. We understand rice, gold, and guns. You are a diplomat. Your career is skyrocket-ing. Now, what would happen if you divorced your wife to marry a Communist Chinese actress?

GALLIMARD. That's not being realistic. That's defeating yourself before you begin.

SONG. We must conserve our strength for the battles we can win.

GALLIMARD. That sounds like a fortune cookie!

SONG. Where do you think fortune cookies come from?

GALLIMARD. I don't care.

SONG. You do. So do I. And we should. That is why I say I'm not worthy. I'm worthy to love and even to be loved by you. But I am not worthy to end the career of one of the West's most promising diplomats.

GALLIMARD. It's not that great a career! I made it sound like more than it is!

SONG. Modesty will get you nowhere. Flatter yourself, and you flatter me. I'm flattered to decline your offer. (*She exits.*)

GALLIMARD. (*To us.*) Butterfly and I argued all night. And, in the end, I left, knowing I would never be her husband. She went away for several months — to the countryside, like a small animal. Until the night I received her call. (*A baby's cry from o.s. Song enters, carrying a child.*)

SONG. He looks like you.

GALLIMARD. Oh! (*Beat; he approaches the baby.*) Well, babies are never very attractive at birth.

SONG. Stop!

GALLIMARD. I'm sure he'll grow more beautiful with age. More like his mother.

SONG. "Chi vide mai/ a bimbo del Giappon . . ."

GALLIMARD. "What baby, I wonder, was ever born in Japan" — or China, for that matter —

SONG. ". . . occhi azzurrini?"

GALLIMARD. "With azure eyes" — they're actually sort of brown, wouldn't you say?

SONG. "E il labbro."

GALLIMARD. "And such lips!" (*He kisses Song.*) And such lips.

SONG. "E i ricciolini d'oro schietto?"

GALLIMARD. "And such a head of golden" — if slightly patchy — "curls?"

SONG. I'm going to call him "Peepee."

GALLIMARD. Darling, could you repeat that because I'm sure a rickshaw just flew by overhead.

SONG. You heard me.

GALLIMARD. "Song Peepee"? May I suggest Michael, or Stephan, or Adolph?

SONG. You may, but I won't listen.

GALLIMARD. You can't be serious. Can you imagine the time this child will have in school?

SONG. In the West, yes.

GALLIMARD. It's worse than naming him Ping Pong or Long Dong or —

SONG. But he's never going to live in the West, is he? (*Pause.*)

GALLIMARD. That wasn't my choice.

SONG. It is mine. And this is my promise to you: I will raise him, he will be our child, but he will never burden you outside of China.

GALLIMARD. Why do you make these promises? I want to be burdened! I want a scandal to cover the papers!

SONG. (*To us.*) Prophetic.

GALLIMARD. I'm serious.

SONG. So am I. His name is as I registered it. And he will never live in the West. (*Song exits with the child.*)

GALLIMARD. (*To us.*) It is possible that her stubbornness only made me want her more. That drawing back at the moment of my capitulation was the most brilliant strategy she could have chosen. It is possible. But it is also possible that by this point she could have said, could have done . . . anything, and I would have adored her still.

SCENE 9

Beijing. 1966.
A driving rhythm of Chinese percussion fills the stage.

GALLIMARD. And then, China began to change. Mao became very old, and his cult became very strong. And, like many old men, he entered his second childhood. So he handed over the reins of state to those with minds like his own. And children ruled the Middle Kingdom with complete caprice. The doctrine of the Cultural Revolution implied continuous anarchy. Contact between Chinese and foreigners became impossible. Our flat was confiscated. Her fame and my money now counted against us. (*Two dancers in Mao suits and red-starred caps enter, and begin crudely mimicking revolutionary violence, in an agitprop fashion.*) And somehow the American war went wrong too. Four hundred thousand dollars were being spent for every Viet Cong killed; so General Westmoreland's remark that the Oriental does not value life the way Americans do was oddly accurate. Why weren't the Vietnamese people giving in? Why were they content instead to die and die and die again? (*Toulon enters. Percussion and dancers continue* U.S.)

TOULON. Congratulations, Gallimard.

GALLIMARD. Excuse me, sir?

TOULON. Not a promotion. That was last time. You're going home.

GALLIMARD. What?

TOULON. Don't say I didn't warn you.

GALLIMARD. I'm being transferred . . . because I was wrong about the American war?

TOULON. Of course not. We don't care about the Americans. We care about your mind. The quality of your analysis. In general, everything you've predicted here in the Orient . . . just hasn't happened.

GALLIMARD. I think that's premature.

TOULON. Don't force me to be blunt. Okay, you said China was ready to open to Western trade. The only thing they're trading out there are Western heads. And, yes, you said the Americans would succeed in Indochina. You were kidding, right?

GALLIMARD. I think the end is in sight.

TOULON. Don't be pathetic. And don't take this personally. You were wrong. It's not your fault.

GALLIMARD. But I'm going home.

TOULON. Right. Could I have the number of your mistress? (*Beat.*) Joke! Joke! Eat a croissant for me. (*Toulon exits. Song, wearing a Mao suit, is dragged in from the wings as part of the* U.S. *dance. They "beat" her, then lampoon the acrobatics of the Chinese opera, as she is made to kneel onstage.*)

GALLIMARD. (*Simultaneously.*) I don't care to recall how Butterfly and I said our hurried farewell. Perhaps it was better to end our affair before it killed her. (*Gallimard Exits. Percussion rises in volume. The lampooning becomes faster, more frenetic. At its height, Comrade Chin walks across the stage with a banner reading: "The Actor Renounces His Decadent Profession!" She reaches the kneeling Song. At the moment Chin touches Song's chin, percussion stops with a thud. Dancers strike poses.*)

CHIN. Actor-oppressor, for years you have lived above the common people and looked down on their labor. While the farmer ate millet—

SONG. I ate pastries from France and sweetmeats from silver trays.

CHIN. And how did you come to live in such an exalted position?

SONG. I was a plaything for the imperialists!

CHIN. What did you do?

SONG. I shamed China by allowing myself to be corrupted by a foreigner . . .

CHIN. What does this mean? The People demand a full confession!

SONG. I engaged in the lowest perversions with China's enemies!

CHIN. What perversions? Be more clear!

SONG. I let him put it up my ass! (*Dancers look over, disgusted.*)

CHIN. Aaaa-ya! How can you use such sickening language?!

SONG. My language . . . is only as foul as the crimes I committed . . .

CHIN. Yeah. That's better. So — what do you want to do . . . now?

SONG. I want to serve the people. (*Percussion starts up, with Chinese strings.*)

CHIN. What?

SONG. I want to serve the people! (*Dancers regain their revolutionary smiles, and begin a dance of victory.*)

CHIN. What?!

SONG. I want to serve the people!! (*Dancers unveil a banner: "The Actor is Re-Habilitated!" Song remains kneeling before Chin, as the dancers bounce around them, then Exit. Music out.*)

SCENE 10

A commune. Hunan Province. 1970.

CHIN. How you planning to do that?

SONG. I've already worked four years in the fields of Hunan, Comrade Chin.

CHIN. So? Farmers work all their lives. Let me see your

hands. (*Song holds them out for her inspection.*) Goddamn! Still so smooth! How long does it take to turn you actors into good anythings? Hunh. You've just spent too many years in luxury to be any good to the Revolution.

SONG. I served the Revolution.

CHIN. Serve the Revolution? Bullshit! You wore dresses! Don't tell me — I was there. I saw you! You and your white vice-consul! Stuck up there in your flat, living off the People's Treasury! Yeah, I knew what was going on! You two . . . homos! Homos! Homos! (*Pause; she composes herself.*) Ah! Well . . . you will serve the people, all right. But not with the Revolution's money. This time, you use your own money.

SONG. I have no money.

CHIN. Shut up! And you won't stink up China anymore with your pervert stuff. You'll pollute the place where pollution begins — the West.

SONG. What do you mean?

CHIN. Shut up! You're going to France. Without a cent in your pocket. You find your consul's house, you make him pay your expenses —

SONG. No.

CHIN. And you give us weekly reports! Useful information!

SONG. That's crazy. It's been four years.

CHIN. Either that, or back to rehabilitation center!

SONG. Comrade Chin, he's not going to support me! Not in France! He's a white man! I was just his plaything —

CHIN. Oh yuck! Again with the sickening language? Where's my stick?

SONG. You don't understand the mind of a man. (*Pause.*)

CHIN. Oh no? No I don't? Then how come I'm married, huh? How come I got a man? Five, six years ago, you always tell me those kind of things, I felt very bad. But not now! Because what does the Chairman say? He tells us *I'm* now the smart one, you're now the nincompoop! *You're* the blockhead, the harebrain, the nitwit! You think you're so smart? You understand "The Mind of a Man"? Good! Then *you* go to France and be a pervert for Chairman Mao! (*Chin and Song exit in opposite directions.*)

Paris. 1968 – 70.
Gallimard Enters.

GALLIMARD. And what was waiting for me back in Paris? Well, better Chinese food than I'd eaten in China. Friends and relatives. A little accounting, regular schedule, keeping track of traffic violations in the suburbs. . . . And the indignity of students shouting the slogans of Chairman Mao at me — in French.

HELGA. Rene? Rene? (*She enters, soaking wet.*) I've had a . . . problem. (*She sneezes.*)

GALLIMARD. You're wet.

HELGA. Yes, I . . . coming back from the grocer's. A group of students, waving red flags, they — (*Gallimard fetches a towel.*) — they ran by, I was caught up along with them. Before I knew what was happening — (*Gallimard gives her the towel.*) Thank you. The police started firing water cannons at us. I tried to shout, to tell them I was the wife of a diplomat, but — you know how it is . . . (*Pause.*) Needless to say, I lost the groceries. Rene, what's happening to France?

GALLIMARD. What's — ? Well, nothing, really.

HELGA. Nothing?! The storefronts are in flames, there's glass in the streets, buildings are toppling — and I'm wet!

GALLIMARD. Nothing! . . . that I care to think about.

HELGA. And is that why you stay in this room?

GALLIMARD. Yes, in fact.

HELGA. With the incense burning? You know something? I hate incense. It smells so sickly sweet.

GALLIMARD. Well, I hate the French. Who just smell — period!

HELGA. And the Chinese were better?

GALLIMARD. Please — don't start.

HELGA. When we left, this exact same thing, the riots —

GALLIMARD. No, no . . .

HELGA. Students screaming slogans, smashing down doors —

56

GALLIMARD. Helga—

HELGA. It was going on in China, too. Don't you remember?!

GALLIMARD. Helga! Please! (*pause*) You have never understood China, have you? You walk in here with these ridiculous ideas, that the West is falling apart, that China was spitting in our faces. You come in, dripping of the streets, and you leave water all over my floor. (*He grabs Helga's towel, begins mopping up the floor.*)

HELGA. But it's the truth!

GALLIMARD. Helga, I want a divorce. (*Pause; Gallimard continues mopping the floor.*)

HELGA. I take it back. China is . . . beautiful. Incense, I like incense.

GALLIMARD. I've had a mistress.

HELGA. So?

GALLIMARD. For eight years.

HELGA. I knew you would. I knew you would the day I married you. And now what? You want to marry her?

GALLIMARD. I can't. She's in China.

HELGA. I see. You know that no one else is ever going to marry me, right?

GALLIMARD. I'm sorry.

HELGA. And you want to leave. For someone who's not here, is that right?

GALLIMARD. That's right.

HELGA. You can't live with her, but still you don't want to live with me.

GALLIMARD. That's right. (*Pause.*)

HELGA. Shit. How terrible that I can figure that out. (*Pause.*) I never thought I'd say it. But, in China, I was happy. I knew, in my own way, I knew that you were not everything you pretended to be. But the pretense—going on your arm to the embassy ball, visiting your office and the guards saying, "Good morning, good morning, Madame Gallimard" —the pretense . . . was very good indeed. (*Pause.*) I hope everyone is mean to you for the rest of your life. (*She exits.*)

GALLIMARD. (*To us.*) Prophetic. (*Marc enters with two drinks; to Marc.*) In China, I was different from all other men.

MARC. Sure. You were white. Here's your drink.

GALLIMARD. I felt . . . touched.

MARC. In the head? Rene, I don't want to hear about the Oriental love goddess. Okay? One night — can we just drink and throw up without a lot of conversation?

GALLIMARD. You still don't believe me, do you?

MARC. Sure I do. She was the most beautiful, et cetera, et cetera, blasé, blasé. (*Pause.*)

GALLIMARD. My life in the West has been such a disappointment.

MARC. Life in the West is like that. You'll get used to it. Look, you're driving me away. I'm leaving. Happy, now? Look, I have a date tomorrow night. You wanna come? I can fix you up with —

GALLIMARD. Of course. I would love to come. (*Pause.*)

MARC. Uh — on second thought, no. You'd better get ahold of yourself first. (*He exits; Gallimard nurses his drink.*)

GALLIMARD. (*To us.*) This is the ultimate cruelty, isn't it? That I can talk and talk and to anyone listening, it's only air — too rich a diet to be swallowed by a mundane world. Why can't anyone understand? That in China, I once loved, and was loved by, very simply, the Perfect Woman. (*Song enters, dressed as Butterfly in wedding kimono. To Song.*) Not again. My imagination is hell. Am I asleep this time? Or did I drink too much?

SONG. Rene?

GALLIMARD. God, it's too painful! That you speak?

SONG. What are you talking about? Rene — touch me.

GALLIMARD. Why?

SONG. I'm real. Take my hand.

GALLIMARD. Why? So you can disappear again and leave me clutching at the air? For the entertainment of my neighbors who — ? (*Song touches Gallimard.*)

SONG. Rene? (*Gallimard takes Song's hand. Silence.*)

GALLIMARD. Butterfly? I never doubted you'd return.

SONG. You hadn't . . . forgotten — ?

GALLIMARD. Yes, actually, I've forgotten everything. My mind, you see — there wasn't enough room in this hard head — not for the world *and* for you. No, there was only room for one. (*Beat.*) Come, look. See? Your bed has been waiting, with the Klimt poster you like, and—see? The xiang lu [incense burner] you gave me?

SONG. I . . . I don't know what to say.

GALLIMARD. There's nothing to say. Not at the end of a long trip. Can I make you some tea?

SONG. But where's your wife?

GALLIMARD. She's by my side. She's by my side at last. (*Gallimard reaches to embrace Song. Song sidesteps, dodging him.*) Why?!

SONG. (*To us.*) So I did return to Renee in Paris. Where I found—

GALLIMARD. Why do you run away? Can't we show them how we embraced that evening?

SONG. Please. I'm talking.

GALLIMARD. You have to do what I say! I'm conjuring you up in my mind!

SONG. Rene, I've never done what you've said. Why should it be any different in your mind? Now split—the story moves on, and I must change.

GALLIMARD. I welcomed you into my home! I didn't have to, you know! I could've left you penniless on the streets of Paris! But I took you in!

SONG. Thank you.

GALLIMARD. So . . . please . . . don't change.

SONG. You know I have to. You know I will. And anyway, what difference does it make? No matter what your eyes tell you, you can't ignore the truth. You already know too much. (*Gallimard exits. Song turns to us.*) The change I'm going to make requires about five minutes. So I thought you might want to take this opportunity to stretch your legs, enjoy a drink, or listen to the musicians. I'll be here, when you return, right where you left me. (*Song goes to a mirror in front of which is a wash basin of water. She starts to remove her makeup as stagelights go to half and houselights come up.*)

ACT THREE

Scene 1

A courthouse in Paris. 1986.
  As he promised, Song has completed the bulk of his transformation onstage by the time the houselights go down and the stagelights come up full. He removes his wig and kimono, leaving them on the floor. Underneath, he wears a well-cut suit.

SONG. So I'd done my job better than I had a right to expect. Well, give him some credit, too. He's right — I was in a fix when I arrived in Paris. I walked from the airport into town, then I located, by blind groping, the Chinatown district. Let me make one thing clear: whatever else may be said about the Chinese, they are stingy! I slept in doorways three days until I could find a tailor who would make me this kimono on credit. As it turns out, maybe I didn't even need it. Maybe he would've been happy to see me in a simple shift and mascara. But . . . better safe than sorry.
  That was 1970, when I arrived in Paris. For the next fifteen years, yes, I lived a very comfy life. Some relief, believe me, after four years on a fucking commune in Nowheresville, China. Rene supported the boy and me, and I did some demonstrations around the country as part of my "cultural exchange" cover. And then there was the spying. (*Song moves* U.S., *to a chair. Toulon enters as a judge, wearing the appropriate wig and robes. He sits near Song. It's 1986, and Song is testifying in a courtroom.*) Not much at first. Rene had lost all his high-level contacts. Comrade Chin wasn't very interested in parking-ticket statistics. But finally, at my urging, Rene got a job as a courier, handling sensitive documents. He'd photograph them for me, and I'd pass them on to the Chinese embassy.
JUDGE. Did he understand the extent of his activity?
SONG. He didn't ask. He knew that I needed those documents, and that was enough.

JUDGE. But he must've known he was passing classified information.

SONG. I can't say.

JUDGE. He never asked what you were going to do with them?

SONG. Nope. (*Pause.*)

JUDGE. There is one thing that the court — indeed, that all of France — would like to know.

SONG. Fire away.

JUDGE. Did Monsieur Gallimard know you were a man?

SONG. Well, he never saw me completely naked. Ever.

JUDGE. But surely, he must've . . . how can I put this?

SONG. Put it however you like. I'm not shy. He must've felt around?

JUDGE. Mmmmm.

SONG. Not really. I did all the work. He just laid back. Of course we did enjoy more . . . complete union, and I suppose he *might* have wondered why I was always on my stomach, but. . . . But what you're thinking is, "Of course a wrist must've brushed . . . a hand hit . . . over twenty years!" Yeah. Well, Your Honor, it was my job to make him think I was a woman. And chew on this: it wasn't all that hard. See, my mother was a prostitute along the Bundt before the Revolution. And, uh, I think it's fair to say she learned a few things about Western men. So I borrowed her knowledge. In service to my country.

JUDGE. Would you care to enlighten the court with this secret knowledge? I'm sure we're all very curious.

SONG. I'm sure you are. (*Pause.*) Okay, Rule One is: Men always believe what they want to hear. So a girl can tell the most obnoxious lies and the guys will believe them every time — "This is my first time" — "That's the biggest I've ever seen" — or *both*, which, if you really think about it, is not possible in a single lifetime. You've maybe heard those phrases a few times in your own life, yes, Your Honor?

JUDGE. It's not my life, Monsieur Song, which is on trial today.

SONG. Okay, okay, just trying to lighten up the proceedings. Tough room.

JUDGE. Go on.

SONG. Rule Two: As soon as a Western man comes into contact with the East — he's already confused. The West has sort of an international rape mentality towards the East. Do you know rape mentality?

JUDGE. Give us your definition, please.

SONG. Basically, "Her mouth says no, but her eyes say yes." The West thinks of itself as masculine—big guns, big industry, big money—so the East is feminine—weak, delicate, poor... but good at art, and full of inscrutable wisdom—the feminine mystique. Her mouth says no, but her eyes say yes. The West believes the East, deep down, *wants* to be dominated—because a woman can't think for herself.

JUDGE. What does this have to do with my question?

SONG. You expect Oriental countries to submit to your guns, and you expect Oriental women to be submissive to your men. That's why you say they make the best wives.

JUDGE. But why would that make it possible for you to fool Monsieur Gallimard? Please — get to the point.

SONG. One, because when he finally met his fantasy woman, he wanted more than anything to believe that she was, in fact, a woman. And second, I am an Oriental. And being an Oriental, I could never be completely a man. (*Pause.*)

JUDGE. Your armchair political theory is tenuous, Monsieur Song.

SONG. You think so? That's why you'll lose in all your dealings with the East.

JUDGE. Just answer my question: did he know you were a man? (*Pause.*)

SONG. You know, Your Honor, I never asked.

SCENE 2

Same.

   Music from the "Death Scene" from Butterfly *blares over the house speakers. It is the loudest thing we've heard in this play.*

62

Gallimard Enters, crawling towards Song's wig and kimono.

GALLIMARD. Butterfly? Butterfly? (*Song remains a man, in the witness box, delivering a testimony we do not hear. To us.*) In my moment of greatest shame, here, in this courtroom — with that . . . person up there, telling the world. . . . What strikes me especially is how shallow he is, how glib and obsequious . . . completely . . . without substance! The type that prowls around discos with a gold medallion stinking of garlic. So little like my Butterfly.

Yet even in this moment my mind remains agile, flip-flopping like a man on a trampoline. Even now, my picture dissolves, and I see that . . . witness . . . talking to me. (*Song suddenly stands straight up in his witness box, and looks at Gallimard.*)

SONG. Yes. You. White man. (*Song steps out of the witness box, and moves D.S. towards Gallimard. Light change.*)

GALLIMARD. (*To Song.*) Who? Me?

SONG. Do you see any other white men?

GALLIMARD. Yes. There're white men all around. This is a French courtroom.

SONG. So you are an adventurous imperialist. Tell me, why did it take you so long? To come back to this place?

GALLIMARD. What place?

SONG. This theatre in China. Where we met many years ago.

GALLIMARD. (*To us.*) And once again, against my will, I am transported. (*Chinese opera music comes up on the speakers. Song begins to do opera moves, as he did the night they met.*)

SONG. Do you remember? The night you gave your heart?

GALLIMARD. It was a long time ago.

SONG. Not long enough. A night that turned your world upside down.

GALLIMARD. Perhaps.

SONG. Oh, be honest with me. What's another bit of flattery when you've already given me twenty years' worth? It's a wonder my head hasn't swollen to the size of China.

GALLIMARD. Who's to say it hasn't?

63

SONG. Who's to say? And what's the shame? In pride? You think I could've pulled this off if I wasn't already full of pride when we met? No, not just pride. Arrogance. It takes arrogance, really — to believe you can will, with your eyes and your lips, the destiny of another. (*He dances.*) C'mon. Admit it. You still want me. Even in slacks and a button-down collar.

GALLIMARD. I don't see what the point of —

SONG. You don't? Well maybe, Rene, just maybe — I want you.

GALLIMARD. You do?

SONG. Then again, maybe I'm just playing with you. How can you tell? (*Reprising his feminine character, he sidles up to Gallimard.*) "How I wish there were even a small cafe to sit in. With men in tuxedos, and cappuccinos, and bad expatriate jazz." Now you want to kiss me, don't you?

GALLIMARD. (*Pulling away.*) What makes you —?

SONG. — so sure? See? I take the words from your mouth. Then I wait for you to come and retrieve them. (*He reclines on the floor.*)

GALLIMARD. Why?! Why do you treat me so cruelly?

SONG. Perhaps I *was* treating you cruelly. But now — I'm being nice. Come here, my little one.

GALLIMARD. I'm not your little one!

SONG. My mistake. It's I who am *your* little one, right?

GALLIMARD. Yes, I —

SONG. So come get your little one. If you like, I may even let you strip me.

GALLIMARD. I mean, you were! Before . . . but not like this!

SONG. I was? Then perhaps I still am. If you look hard enough. (*He starts to remove his clothes.*)

GALLIMARD. What — what are you doing?

SONG. Helping you to see through my act.

GALLIMARD. Stop that! I don't want to! I don't —

SONG. Oh, but you asked me to strip, remember?

GALLIMARD. What? That was years ago! And I took it back!

SONG. No. You postponed it. Postponed the inevitable. Today, the inevitable has come calling. (*From the speakers, cacophony:* Butterfly *mixed in with Chinese gongs.*)

GALLIMARD. No! Stop! I don't want to see!

SONG. Then look away.

GALLIMARD. You're only in my mind! All this is in my mind! I order you! To stop!

SONG. To what? To strip? That's just what I'm —

GALLIMARD. No! Stop! I want you —!

SONG. You want me?

GALLIMARD. To stop!

SONG. You know something, Rene? Your mouth says no, but your eyes say yes. Turn them away. I dare you.

GALLIMARD. I don't have to! Every night, you say you're going to strip, but then I beg you and you stop!

SONG. I guess tonight is different.

GALLIMARD. Why? Why should that be?

SONG. Maybe I've become frustrated. Maybe I'm saying "Look at me, you fool!" Or maybe I'm just feeling . . . sexy. (*He is down to his briefs.*)

GALLIMARD. Please. This is unnecessary. I know what you are.

SONG. You do? What am I?

GALLIMARD. A — a man.

SONG. You don't really believe that.

GALLIMARD. Yes I do! I knew all the time somewhere that my happiness was temporary, my love a deception. But my mind kept the knowledge at bay. To make the wait bearable.

SONG. Monsieur Gallimard — the wait is over. (*Song drops his briefs. He is naked. Sound cue out. Slowly, we and Song come to the realization that what we had thought to be Gallimard's sobbing is actually his laughter.*)

GALLIMARD. Oh god! What an idiot! Of course!

SONG. Rene — what?

GALLIMARD. Look at you! You're a man! (*He bursts into laughter again.*)

SONG. I fail to see what's so funny!

GALLIMARD. "You fail to see —!" I mean, you never did have much of a sense of humor, did you? I just think it's ridiculously funny that I've wasted so much time on just a man!

SONG. Wait. I'm not "just a man."

GALLIMARD. No? Isn't that what you've been trying to convince me of?

SONG. Yes, but what I mean —

GALLIMARD. And now, I finally believe you, and you tell me it's not true? I think you must have some kind of identity problem.

SONG. Will you listen to me?

GALLIMARD. Why?! I've been listening to you for twenty years. Don't I deserve a vacation?

SONG. I'm not just any man!

GALLIMARD. Then, what exactly are you?

SONG. Rene, how can you ask —? Okay, what about this? (*He picks up Butterfly's robes, starts to dance around. No music.*)

GALLIMARD. Yes, that's very nice. I have to admit. (*Song holds out his arm to Gallimard.*)

SONG. It's the same skin you've worshiped for years. Touch it.

GALLIMARD. Yes, it does feel the same.

SONG. Now — close your eyes. (*Song covers Gallimard's eyes with one hand. With the other, Song draws Gallimard's hand up to his face. Gallimard, like a blind man, lets his hands run over Song's face.*)

GALLIMARD. This skin, I remember. The curve of her face, the softness of her cheek, her hair against the back of my hand . . .

SONG. I'm your Butterfly. Under the robes, beneath everything, it was always me. Now, open your eyes and admit it — you adore me. (*He removes his hand from Gallimard's eyes.*)

GALLIMARD. You, who knew every inch of my desires — how could you, of all people, have made such a mistake?

SONG. What?

GALLIMARD. You showed me your true self. When all I loved was the lie. A perfect lie, which you let fall to the ground — and now, it's old and soiled.

SONG. So — you never really loved me? Only when I was playing a part?

GALLIMARD. I'm a man who loved a woman created by a man. Everything else — simply falls short. (*Pause.*)

SONG. What am I supposed to do now?

GALLIMARD. You were a fine spy, Monsieur Song, with an

66

even finer accomplice. But now I believe you should go. Get out of my life!

SONG. Go where? Rene, you can't live without me. Not after twenty years.

GALLIMARD. I certainly can't live with you — not after twenty years of betrayal.

SONG. Don't be so stubborn! Where will you go?

GALLIMARD. I have a date . . . with my Butterfly.

SONG. So, throw away your pride. And come . . .

GALLIMARD. Get away from me! Tonight, I've finally learned to tell fantasy from reality. And, knowing the difference, I choose fantasy.

SONG. *I'm* your fantasy!

GALLIMARD. You? You're as real as hamburger. Now get out! I have a date with my Butterfly and I don't want your body polluting the room! (*He tosses Song's suit at him.*) Look at these — you dress like a pimp.

SONG. Hey! These are Armani slacks and — ! (*He puts on his briefs and slacks.*) Let's just say . . . I'm disappointed in you, Rene. In the crush of your adoration, I though you'd become something more. More like . . . a woman.

But no. Men. You're like the rest of them. It's all in the way we dress, and make up our faces, and bat our eyelashes. You really have so little imagination!

GALLIMARD. You, Monsieur Song? Accuse me of too little imagination? You, if anyone, should know — I am pure imagination. And in imagination I will remain. Now get out! (*Gallimard bodily removes Song from the stage, taking his kimono.*)

SONG. Rene! I'll never put on those robes again! You'll be sorry!

GALLIMARD. (*To Song.*) I'm already sorry! (*Looking at the kimono in his hands.*) Exactly as sorry . . . as a Butterfly.

Scene 3

M. Gallimard's prison cell. Paris. 1988.

GALLIMARD. I've played out the events of my life night after night, always searching for a new ending to my story, one where I leave this cell and return forever to my Butter-fly's arms.

Tonight I realize my search is over. That I've looked all along in the wrong place. And now, to you, I will prove that my love was not in vain — by returning to the world of fantasy where I first met her. (*He picks up the kimono; dancers enter.*) There is a vision of the Orient that I have. Of slender women in chong sams and kimonos who die for the love of unworthy foreign devils. Who are born and raised to be the perfect women. Who take whatever punishment we give them, and bounce back, strengthened by love, unconditionally. It is a vision that has become my life. (*Dancers help him make up his face.*) In public, I have continued to deny that Song Liling is a man. This brings me headlines, and is a source of great embarrassment to my French colleagues, who can now be sent into a coughing fit by the mere mention of Chinese food. But alone, in my cell, I have long since faced the truth.

And the truth demands a sacrifice. For mistakes made over the course of a lifetime. My mistakes were simple and absolute — the man I loved was a cad, a bounder. He deserved nothing but a kick in the behind, and instead I gave him . . . all my love.

Yes — love. Why not admit it all? That was my undoing, wasn't it? Love warped my judgment, blinded my eyes, rearranged the very lines on my face . . . until I could look in the mirror and see nothing but . . . a woman. (*Dancers help him put on the Butterfly wig.*) I have a vision. Of the Orient. That, deep within its almond eyes, there are still women. Women willing to sacrifice themselves for the love of a man. Even a man whose love is completely without worth. (*Dancers assist Gallimard in donning the kimono. They hand him a knife.*) Death with honor is better than life . . . life with dishonor. (*He sets himself c.s., in a seppuku position.*) The love of a Butter-fly can withstand many things — unfaithfulness, loss, even abandonment. But how can it face the one sin that implies all others? The devastating knowledge that, underneath it all, the object of her love was nothing more, nothing less than . . . a man. (*He sets the tip of the knife against his body.*) It is 1988. And I have found her at last. In a prison on the outskirts of Paris. My name is Rene Gallimard—also known as **Madame Butterfly.** (*Gallimard turns* U.S. *and plunges the knife into his body, as music from the "Love Duet" blares over the speakers. He collapses into the arms of the dancers, who lay him reverently on the floor. The image holds for several beats. Then a tight special up on Song, who stands as a man, staring at the fallen Gallimard. He smokes a cigarette; the smoke filters up through the lights. Two words leave his lips.*)

SONG. Butterfly? Butterfly? (*Smoke rises as lights fade slowly to black.*)

END OF PLAY

ACT I

Scene Breakdown

ACT/SCENE	Name	
1-1	*GALLIMARD'S PRISON CELL* Song Gallimard 2 Kurogo	Paris 1988
1-2	*A PARTY* WOMAN at Party MAN #1 at Party MAN #2 at Party 2 Kurogo	1988
1-3	*GALLIMARD'S CELL* Gallimard/Pinkerton Marc/Sharpless 2 Kurogo	
1-4	*ECOLE NATIONAL* (Aix-en-Provence) Gallimard Marc 2 Kurogo	1947
1-5	*GALLIMARD'S CELL* Helga Gallimard Song Girl in the Centerfold Suzuki Marc/Sharpless 2 Kurogo	

1-6	*GERMAN AMBASSADOR'S HOUSE* Party People (Same as 1-2) Gallimard Marc Toulon Song 1 Musician (Violin)	Peiking 1960
1-7	*GALLIMARD'S APARTMENT* Gallimard Helga	Peiking 1960
1-8	*CHINESE OPERA HOUSE AND STREET* Gallimard Song Lead Opera Dancer 2 Kurogo (as Dancers)	Peiking 1960
1-9	*GALLIMARD'S BEDROOM AND STREET* Helga Gallimard Song Marc	Peiking 1960
1-10	*SONG'S APARTMENT* Song Gallimard Shu-Fang	Peiking 1960
1-11	*THE FRENCH EMBASSY* Gallimard Marc Song	Peiking 1960

| 1-12 | *AMBASSADOR TOULON RESIDENCE* | Peiking 1960 |

Gallimard
Toulon

| 1-13 | *SONG'S APARTMENT* | Peiking 1960 |

Song
Gallimard

ACT II

| 2-1 | *GALLIMARD'S CELL* | Paris 1988 |

Gallimard

| 2-2 | *GALLIMARD AND BUTTERFLY FLAT* | Peiking 1960 |

Song
Gallimard

| 2-3 | *FRENCH EMBASSY* | Peiking 1966 |

Gallimard
Toulon
Song
Comrade Chin

| 2-4 | *GALLIMARD AND BUTTERFLY FLAT* | Peiking 1966 |

Song
Comrade Chin
Gallimard

| 2-5 | *PEIKING 1961–1963* |

Gallimard
Song
Helga

| 2-6 | *AUSTRIAN EMBASSY PARTY* | Peiking 1963 |

Gallimard

Renee
Party People (Same as 1-2)
Song
Toulon

| 2-7 | GALLIMARD AND BUTTERFLY FLAT | Peiking 1963 |

GALLIMARD AND
*   BUTTERFLY FLAT*   Peiking 1963
Song
Comrade Chin
Gallimard

2-8   *SAME AS ABOVE*
Gallimard
Song

2-9   *PEIKING 1966*
Gallimard
Toulon
Comrade Chin
Song

2-10   *A COMMUNE, HUNAN*   1970
           PROVINCE
Comrade Chin
Song
2 Kurogo (As Mao
   Soldiers)

2-11   *PARIS*   1968–1970
Gallimard
Helga
Marc
Song
2 Kurogo

          ACT III
3-1   *A COURTHOUSE IN*   1986
          PARIS
Song
Judge

3-2   *SAME*
Gallimard
Song

3-3   *GALLIMARD'S CELL*   Paris 1988
Gallimard
2 Kurogo

RUNNING PROP LIST

PRE-SET:

2 arm chairs
2 armless chairs
2 stool/tables
1 bench
4 down stage screens off stage Left
4 up stage screens off stage Left
Rolled NAGASAKI banner up Stage Center
Portable tape recorder on bench Center
5 "girlie" magazines in box on pit rail

STAGE LEFT PROP TABLE:

Naval officer's cap (Gallimard)
Ash tray
French newspaper
Tennis racket
White flower bouquet
Chinese scissors

UP STAGE PROP TABLE:

2 foreign telephones
2 practical (battery operated) Chinese lamps
1 picture in silver frame
1 bowl of flowers
1 stool/table
1 small Chinese vase with flowers

All Peking Opera props:
    6 spears
    2 swords

1 sword and scabbard (Song)
1 duster (Song)
Towel (costume) (Renee)
Hair brush
2 Chinese vases with white flower arrangements
2 Chinese vases with autumn flower arrangements
Leather folder with 6 letters
Desk set: desk blotter, pen and holder
Large official rubber stamp
2 whips (Kurogo)
1 shiang lu (incense holder with incense sticks)
1 red bull horn (Chin)
2 claret glasses (Marc)
1 bottle of expensive wine (Marc)
Note book and pen (Chin)

CENTER PROP TABLE: Tea tray with 2 covered cups and saucers and tea pot
Infant baby doll (Song)

4 silver trays:
  1 silver tray with Champagne bottle and 1 champagne glass filled with ginger ale.
  1 silver tray with Champagne bottle and 2 Champagne glasses filled with ginger ale.
  1 silver tray with fancy liquor bottle and two glasses
  1 silver tray with filled

| | Champagne bottle and two tulip glasses |
| | 1 tennis racket |

PIT PROP TABLE: French newspaper
Critic's critique leaflet
1 flower (Suzuki)
Towel (Gallimard)
Hara-kiri knife (Suzuki)
2 glasses with scotch (tea + water)

PERSONAL PROPS: Cigarette holder (girl at a party)
Cigarette case with lighter and cigarettes (Song)
French cigarettes and lighter (Gallimard)
Cigars, lighter and clipper (Toulon)
Assorted fans to match costumes (Song)
Fan (Suzuki)
Brass telescope (small) (Song)

ACT III MAKE-UP CHANGE PROPS: Make-up table with mirror and battery operated light (store up stage off Left) with: pot of "Sea Breeze" make-up remover, chamois, cotton balls, Q-tips, spray bottle with water, comb, wig block hari-kiri knife, tray of make-up with brushes for white and red and black make-up.

COSTUME PLOT

GALLIMARD

ACT I

Scenes 1+2:
Grey pajamas
Grey T-shirt
Grey cardigan sweater
Grey slippers
Scene 3:
Add: "Pinkerton" naval hat
Scene 4-6:
Creme suit
Creme shirt
Creme bow tie
Creme shoes
Scene 7:
Repeat shirt, pants, shoes
Black/white plaid double-
breasted jacket
Maroon tie
Scene 8-13:
Repeat shirt pants, shoes
Grey robe
Creme suit coat
Gold tie

ACT II:

Scenes 1-9:
Creme suit ensemble
Scene 11:
Repeat Act I Scene 1

ACT III:

Scene 2:
Same

Scene 3:
   Distressed "Butterfly"
   kimono
   Wig

SONG LILING

ACT I:
   Scene 1:
   Peacock ensemble fan
   Scene 5:
   Yellow "Butterfly" ensemble
   Telescope and fan
   white "Butterfly"
   ensemble
   Fan and knife
   Scene 6:
   Repeat White "Butterfly"
   ensemble
   Scene 8:
   "White Snake" ensemble
   Blue Chinese robe
   Blue satin shoes
   Purse, cigarette case, lighter,
   cigarettes.
   Scene 9:
   Pink kimono with sash
   Black slip
   Pink pumps
   Scene 10:
   Black slip
   Black 20's dress
   Black pumps
   Scene 11:
   Yellow kimono ensemble
   Scene 13:
   Grey slip
   Pink kimono

ACT II:
Scene 1:
Purple cheong Sam
Purple pumps
Cloisonne earrings
Scene 2-4:
Same
Scene 5:
Ivory negligee
Ivory chiffon robe
Scene 6:
Ivory Negligee
Peach Satin Robe
Ivory mules
Scene 7:
Ivory nightgown
Ivory chiffon robe
Scene 9:
2 piece Mao suit
Green cap, green socks, green
shoes.
Scene 11:
White kimono
Blue suit
Creme silk shirt
Black shoes, black socks
Purple tie + handkerchief

ACT III:
Scene 1-3:
Distressed "Butterfly"
kimono

MARC / SHARPLESS

ACT I:
Scene 1:
Creme suit
Creme shirt
Creme bow tie
Creme shoes

Scene 3:
  Tan linen jacket
  Striped tie
  Straw fedora
Scene 4:
  Beige tennis sweater
Scene 5:
  Repeat Scene 2
Scene 6:
  Creme suit jacket
  Black tux pants
  Black cummerbund + bow tie
  Black shoes
Scene 9:
  Nightshirt and cap
  Slippers
Scene 11:
  Grey suit
  White shirt
  Blue striped tie
  Black shoes

ACT II:
  Scene 6:
    Repeat Act I Scene 6
  Scene 11:
    Black sweater
    Black corduroy pants
    Black shoes

TOULON / JUDGE

ACT I:
  Scene 1:
    Creme suit
    Creme shirt
    Creme cummerbund and bow
      tie
    Creme shoes
  Scene 6:
    Creme dinner jacket

81

                    Black tux pants
                    Black cummerbund and bow
                        tie
                    Black shoes
                Scene 12:
                    Same

        ACT II:
            Scene 2-3:
                Grey suit
                White shirt
                Burgundy bow tie
                Black shoes
            Scene 6:
                Repeat Act I, Scene 6
            Scene 9:
                Repeat grey suit

        ACT III:
            Scene 1:
                Judge's robe and dickey
                Judge's hat

NOTE: THE FRENCH LEGION OF HONOR RIBBON IS WORN ON ALL TOULON'S JACKETS.

HELGA

                    ACT I:
                    Scene 5 + 7
                        Green suit
                        Green shoes
                    Scene 9:
                        Beige robe
                        Slippers
                    ACT II:
                    Scene 5:
                        Mauve suit
                        Tan pumps
                    Scene 11:
                        Blue skirt and blouse

Trench coat (distressed to
look like it is wet)
Tan pumps
Tan shoulder bag

RENEE

ACT I:
Scene 1:
Creme dress
Creme hat
Creme pumps
Scene 5:
Negligee
Mules
Scene 6:
Long black gown
Black hat
Black pumps

ACT II:
Scene 6:
Long purple dress
Purple shoes
Pink wrap towel

COMRADE CHIN / SUZUKI / SHU FANG
ACT I:
Scene 5:
Mao suit
Kimono (grey)
Green suit
Scene 10:
Mao suit
Chinese tunic
Green shoes
ACT II:
Scene 3,4,7,
9,10:
Mao suit
Green shoes

KUROGO / WARRIOR / RED BRIGADE
ACT I
Scene 1-7:
- Kurogo suit
- Black gloves
- Black Chinese shoes

Scene 8:
- Warrior costume (silver)
- Black "monkey" shoes
- Black robe

Scenes 9-13:
- Repeat Kurogo costume

ACT II:
Scenes 1-9:
- Same

Scene 10:
- Red brigade uniform
- Green Chinese shoes

Scene 11:
- Repeat Kurogo costume

ACT III:
Scenes 1-3:
- Same

It all started in May of 1986, over casual dinner conversation. A friend asked, had I heard about the French diplomat who'd fallen in love with a Chinese actress, who subsequently turned out to be not only a spy, but a man? I later found a two paragraph story in the New York *Times*. The diplomat, Bernard Bouriscot, attempting to account for the fact that he had never seen his "girlfriend" naked, was quoted as saying, "I thought she was very modest. I thought it was a Chinese custom."

Now, I am aware that this is *not* a Chinese custom, that Asian women are no more shy with their lovers than are women of the West. I am also aware, however, that Bouriscot's assumption was consistent with a certain stereotyped view of Asians as bowing, blushing flowers. I therefore concluded that the diplomat must have fallen in love, not with a person, but with a fantasy stereotype. I also inferred that, to the extent the Chinese spy encouraged these misperceptions, he must have played up to an exploited this image of the Oriental woman as demure and submissive. (In general, by the way, we prefer the term "Asian" to "Oriental," in the same way "Black" is superior to "Negro." I use the term "Oriental" specifically to denote an exotic or imperialistic view of the East.)

I suspected there was a play here. I purposely refrained from further research, for I was not interested in writing docudrama. Frankly, I didn't want the "truth" to interfere with my own speculations. I told Stuart Ostrow, a producer with whom I'd worked before, that I envisioned the story as a musical. I remember going so far as to speculate that it could be some "great *Madame Butterfly*-like tragedy." Stuart was very intrigued, and encouraged me with some early funding.

Before I can begin writing, I must "break the back of the story," and find some angle which compels me to set pen to

paper. I was driving down Santa Monica Blvd. one after-
noon, and asked myself, "What did Bouriscot think he was
getting in this Chinese actress?" The answer came to me
clearly: "He probably thought he had found Madame
Butterfly."

The idea of doing a deconstructivist *Madama Butterfly* immediately appealed to me. This, despite the fact that I didn't
even know the plot of the opera! I knew Butterfly only as a
cultural stereotype; speaking of an Asian woman, we would
sometimes say, "She's pulling a Butterfly," which meant
playing the submissive Oriental number. Yet, I felt con-
vinced that the libretto would include yet another lotus blossom pining away for a cruel Caucasian man, and dying for
her love. Such a story has become too much of a cliche not to
be included in the archetypal East-West romance that started
it all. Sure enough, when I purchased the record, I discovered it contained a wealth of sexist and racist cliches, reaf-
firming my faith in Western culture.

Very soon after, I came up with the basic "arc" of my play:
the Frenchman fantasizes that he is Pinkerton and his lover is
Butterfly. By the end of the piece, he realizes that it is he who
has been Butterfly, in that the Frenchman has been duped by
love; the Chinese spy, who exploited that love, is therefore
the real Pinkerton. I wrote a proposal to Stuart Ostrow, who
found it very exciting. (On the night of the Tony Awards,
Stuart produced my original two-page treatment, and we
were gratified to see that it was, indeed, the play I eventually
wrote.)

I wrote a play, rather than a musical, because, having "broken the back" of the story, I wanted to start immediately and
not be hampered by the lengthy process of collaboration. I
would like to think, however, that the play has retained many
of its musical roots. I sent it to Stuart as a courtesy, assuming
he would not be interested in producing what had become a
straight play. Instead, he flew out to Los Angeles immediately for script conferences. Coming from a background in
the not-for-profit theatre, I suggested that we develop the

work at a regional institution. Stuart, nothing if not bold, argued for bringing it directly to Broadway.

It was also Stuart who suggested John Dexter to direct. I had known Dexter's work only by its formidable reputation. Stuart sent the script to John, who called back the next day, saying it was the best play he'd read in twenty years. Naturally, this predisposed me to like him a great deal. We met in December in New York. Not long after, we persuaded Eiko Ishioka to design our sets and costumes. I had admired her work from afar ever since, as a college student, I had seen her poster for *Apocalypse Now* in Japan. By January, 1987, Stuart had optioned *M. Butterfly*, Dexter was signed to direct, and the normally sloth-like pace of commercial theatre had been given a considerable prod.

On January 4, 1988, we commenced rehearsals. I was very pleased that John Lithgow had agreed to play the French diplomat, who I named Rene Gallimard. Throughout his tenure with us, Lithgow was every inch the center of our company, intelligent and professional, passionate and generous. B.D. Wong was forced to endure a 5-month audition period before we selected him to play Song Liling. Watching B. D.'s growth was one of the joys of the rehearsal process, as he constantly attained higher levels of performance. As we proceeded with our work, I realized that we had been fortunate enough to put together a company with not only great talent, but also wonderful camaraderie.

We opened in Washington, D.C. at the National Theatre, where *West Side Story* and *Amadeus* had premiered. On the morning after opening night, most of the reviews were glowing, except for The Washington *Post*. Throughout our run in Washington, Stuart never pressured us to make the play more "commercial" in reaction to that review. We all simply concluded that the gentleman was possibly insecure about his own sexual orientation and therefore found the play threatening. And we continued our work.

Once we opened in New York, the play found a life of its

own. I suppose the most gratifying thing for me is that we had never compromised to be more "Broadway;" we simply did the work we thought best. That our endeavor should be rewarded to the degree it has is one of those all-too-rare instances when one's own perception and that of the world are in agreement.

SPECIFIC NOTES TO DIRECTORS AND ACTORS

I include here some thoughts directed at those who might want to do future productions of *M. Butterfly*. In general, my attitude is that those who perform the play after its initial production should have relatively free rein to pursue their own interpretations. This allows for greater artistic freedom, and may result in approaches I had not personally envisioned, but which may further illuminate the play. Nevertheless, as general guidelines, I have set down a few of my own opinions.

CASTING

Clearly, the role of Song Liling is the most difficult to cast. When we first started looking for Broadway, our excellent casting directors, Meg Simon and Fran Kumin, laughed about having to find "a Chinese transvestite who can sing and dance." I am of the opinion that Song should unquestionably be played by an Asian actor, and preferably a man.

With regard to the former, the age of Caucasian actors playing Charlie Chan has hopefully been banished into our B-movie past (despite a recent attempt by Peter Ustinov to revive this not-so-honorable tradition). The fact is, we are not yet in a society color-blind enough to provide for equal opportunity in acting roles. It is so difficult for actors of color to find decent roles that it seems immoral to deny them those few which are available. Furthermore, as so much of the play concerns the relationship of East and West, it would be self-defeating to cast two Westerners.

I realize that in certain parts of the country, Asian actors of any variety, let alone one with the multiplicity of talents required by the role, may be difficult to find. In this case, I would kindly request that you contact my representatives through Dramatists Play Service, and explain your situation.

The issue of whether Song should be played by a man or a woman is somewhat more subtle. I believe Song should be a man for many reasons, not least of which is the fact that the character disrobes completely in Act III, Scene 2, and the use of prosthetic devices in the theatre is still rather uncommon (More on nudity later). Furthermore, it seems to me that casting a woman is not playing fair with the audience. If they are to believe that Gallimard was seduced by a man disguised as a woman, then we have, I would think, the obligation to present an actor doing exactly that. Finally, I feel the other choice runs the risk of exploiting the very sexual oppression it seeks to condemn, in the same fashion as violent movies that pretend to be anti-violence. If a woman plays Song, then we are watching a woman being oppressed in a very seductive and pleasurable manner. If Gallimard is actually oppressing a man, the effect on an audience is much more subversive.

The other parts are fairly straightforward in terms of casting. In John Dexter's production, the two Dancers (or "kurogo," the Kabuki term for "invisible" stagehands) were male, and we employed a third Dancer, the extraordinary Peking Opera star Jamie H. J. Guan, to add authenticity and acrobatics to the Opera excerpt in Act I, Scene 8. The parts could also be cast, of course, with simply one Asian male and one Asian female.

SET AND COSTUMES

Certainly an important element of the Broadway production's success was the "look" of our show. Unfortunately, I cannot take credit for it. On writing the play, I had no idea whether it would best be realized by a series of different settings indicated by backdrops (as in, for instance, the Broadway production of David Hare's *Plenty*), or by some very ingenious unit set.

Eiko and Dexter settled upon the latter, to brilliant effect. Eiko's set consisted of a curved ramp which began some twelve feet off the ground in the extreme downstage left corner, and transversed the upstage wall of the stage before enclosing the set in its downstage right corner, then descending into a vomitorium. Behind the ramp was a brilliant red scrim; centerstage was a black raised playing area. Red shoji-like screens ran across the stage in two rows, and could be arranged in various combinations.

While this set wonderfully conveyed the meeting and clash of East and West, of male and female, there has always been a school of thought which argued that the piece could also play effectively on a simple bare stage, in stark Brechtian fashion. While I would be curious to see this approach taken in some future production, I feel that it has some drawbacks. The primary of these being, that *M. Butterfly* is as much about cultural domination as it is racial or sexual. We in the West have a certain "vision of the Orient" which revels in exotica and lush beauty. Again, it seems to me more subversive to present this *chinoiserie* in its full glory, and *then* to question the reasons for the audience taking pleasure.

These observations of course apply also to the show's costumes, again made beautifully for our production by Ms. Ishioka.

MUSIC

The excerpts from *Madama Butterfly* noted in the text of the play are suggestions only. John Dexter's impressive career in opera made it foolish not to rely on his knowledge of Puccini. Consequently, some of the taped opera excerpts he used were the ones I specified, others were different. In general, we seemed to find that it was difficult to underscore spoken dialogue from the play with sung dialogue from the opera. Consequently, the bulk of Dexter's choices involved instrumental sections.

In the Broadway production, we also employed live musicians. Lucia Hwong, a successful and distinguished recording artist in her own right, has composed and served as musical director for my plays from the beginning of my career. She used an ensemble of three musicians: herself on Pipa (Chinese lute); Yukio Tsuji on percussion, shakuhachi (Japanese flute), and guitar; and Jason Hwang (no relation to any of the rest of us Wong/Hwang/Hwongs) on violin and percussion. While future productions are of course free to compose their own music, Ms. Hwong does add a very special understanding and sensibility to my work, and I would recommend that one at least listen to her score, available on tape through Dramatists Play Service.

CHINESE OPERA

As I mentioned before, we were lucky enough to acquire the services of Jamie H. J. Guan who, with his wife, Michelle Ehlers, choreographed our show. Peking Opera is a very old and intricate form, of which I, frankly, know very little. It is therefore essential that anyone wanting to produce *M. Butterfly* hire a Peking Opera teacher/consultant.

One further note: as I mentioned before, *Butterfly* rehearsals began January 4, 1988. However, rehearsals for B.D. and the Dancers had begun several weeks before. This is something for which extra time must unquestionably be provided. In some of my previous plays utilizing Peking Opera, we would devote the first hour or two of every rehearsal day to Opera drills. If it's not done right, it looks very silly.

SONG'S MAKE-UP CHANGE

One of the most effective segments of the play is the break between Acts II and III, where, with the house lights up, Song performs his transformation from woman into man. The fascination of this moment is obvious in the fact that, though the audience is invited to get up, on Broadway it was a rare evening where even a couple of individuals would actually leave their seats.

In Dexter's production, the make-up change was staged against a live musical performance, which gives the audience something else to look at if it happens to be taking a long time for Song to remove his foundation.

NUDITY

There are two nude scenes. In Act I, Renee plays a pin-up girl and strips. On Broadway, where the talented Lindsay Frost originated the role, we placed her underneath the downstage left ramp, where she could be lit behind a scrim. I suppose, if nudity is likely to provoke a jail sentence in your community, it might be reasonable to provide the actress with a body suit. Obviously, however, I prefer total nudity where possible; it sets a very "anything goes" precedent early in the play, and nicely balances the nudity to come in Act III.

I have not personally thought of a way around Song's nudity (this does not, of course, preclude the possibility that one exists). This is the moment in the play where all of Gallimard's illusions are literally stripped away, and anything less (or more, as the case may be) seems to diminish the gesture. Dexter staged the moment with Gallimard on the ramp, upstage center. Song was downstage center, facing us, until the very instant when he drops his boxers, at which point he turns upstage. Consequently, what we see is not Song's weenie, but Gallimard's reaction to it. This seems to me an eminently sensible approach to the scene. As Dexter put it, "If you have Alfred Lunt standing next to a penis, we are not likely to be looking at Mr. Lunt."

ON THAT NOTE, WE CLOSE

I hope you have a rewarding time staging *M. Butterfly*. I'd like to think that the play leaves ample opportunity for talented directors to fully exercise their creativity. I'm very grateful to Stuart Ostrow, John Dexter, Eiko Ishioka, and our first-rate cast, crew, and staff, all of whom played an important part in the text you have before you.

David Henry Hwang
September, 1988

NEW PLAYS

★ **THE EXONERATED by Jessica Blank and Erik Jensen.** Six interwoven stories paint a picture of an American criminal justice system gone horribly wrong and six brave souls who persevered to survive it. "The #1 play of the year...intense and deeply affecting..." –*NY Times.* "Riveting. Simple, honest storytelling that demands reflection." –*A.P.* "Artful and moving...pays tribute to the resilience of human hearts and minds." –*Variety.* "Stark...riveting...cunningly orchestrated." –*The New Yorker.* "Hard-hitting, powerful, and socially relevant." –*Hollywood Reporter.* [7M, 3W] ISBN: 0-8222-1946-8

★ **STRING FEVER by Jacquelyn Reingold.** Lily juggles the big issues: turning forty, artificial insemination and the elusive scientific Theory of Everything in this Off-Broadway comedy hit. "Applies the elusive rules of string theory to the conundrums of one woman's love life. Think *Sex and the City* meets *Copenhagen.*" –*NY Times.* "A funny offbeat and touching look at relationships...an appealing romantic comedy populated by oddball characters." –*NY Daily News.* "Where kooky, zany, and madcap meet...whimsically winsome." –*NY Magazine.* "STRING FEVER will have audience members happily stringing along." –*TheaterMania.com.* "Reingold's language is surprising, inventive, and unique." –*nytheatre.com.* "...[a] whimsical comic voice." –*Time Out.* [3M, 3W (doubling)] ISBN: 0-8222-1952-2

★ **DEBBIE DOES DALLAS adapted by Erica Schmidt, composed by Andrew Sherman, conceived by Susan L. Schwartz.** A modern morality tale told as a comic musical of tragic proportions as the classic film is brought to the stage. "A scream! A saucy, tongue-in-cheek romp." –*The New Yorker.* "Hilarious! DEBBIE manages to have it all: beauty, brains and a great sense of humor!" –*Time Out.* "Shamelessly silly, shrewdly self-aware and proud of being naughty. Great fun!" –*NY Times.* "Racy and raucous, a lighthearted, fast-paced thoroughly engaging and hilarious send-up." –*NY Daily News.* [3M, 5W] ISBN: 0-8222-1955-7

★ **THE MYSTERY PLAYS by Roberto Aguirre-Sacasa.** Two interrelated one acts, loosely based on the tradition of the medieval mystery plays. "... stylish, spine-tingling...Mr. Aguirre-Sacasa uses standard tricks of horror stories, borrowing liberally from masters like Kafka, Lovecraft, Hitchcock...But his mastery of the genre is his own...irresistible." –*NY Times.* "Undaunted by the special-effects limitations of theatre, playwright and *Marvel* comic-book writer Roberto Aguirre-Sacasa maps out some creepy twilight zones in THE MYSTERY PLAYS, an engaging, related pair of one acts...The theatre may rarely deliver shocks equivalent to, say, *Dawn of the Dead,* but Aguirre-Sacasa's work is fine compensation." –*Time Out.* [4M, 2W] ISBN: 0-8222-2038-5

★ **THE JOURNALS OF MIHAIL SEBASTIAN by David Auburn.** This epic one-man play spans eight tumultuous years and opens a uniquely personal window on the Romanian Holocaust and the Second World War. "Powerful." –*NY Times.* "[THE JOURNALS OF MIHAIL SEBASTIAN] allows us to glimpse the idiosyncratic effects of that awful history on one intelligent, pragmatic, recognizably real man..." –*NY Newsday.* [3M, 5W] ISBN: 0-8222-2006-7

★ **LIVING OUT by Lisa Loomer.** The story of the complicated relationship between a Salvadoran nanny and the Anglo lawyer she works for. "A stellar new play. Searingly funny." –*The New Yorker.* "Both generous and merciless, equally enjoyable and disturbing." –*NY Newsday.* "A bitingly funny new comedy. The plight of working mothers is explored from two pointedly contrasting perspectives in this sympathetic, sensitive new play." –*Variety.* [2M, 6W] ISBN: 0-8222-1994-8

DRAMATISTS PLAY SERVICE, INC.
440 Park Avenue South, New York, NY 10016 212-683-8960 Fax 212-213-1539
postmaster@dramatists.com   www.dramatists.com

NEW PLAYS

★ **MATCH by Stephen Belber.** Mike and Lisa Davis interview a dancer and choreographer about his life, but it is soon evident that their agenda will either ruin or inspire them—and definitely change their lives forever. "Prolific laughs and ear-to-ear smiles." –*NY Magazine.* "Uproariously funny, deeply moving, enthralling theater. Stephen Belber's MATCH has great beauty and tenderness, and abounds in wit." –*NY Daily News.* "Three and a half out of four stars." –*USA Today.* "A theatrical steeplechase that leads straight from outrageous bitchery to unadorned, heartfelt emotion." –*Wall Street Journal.* [2M, 1W] ISBN: 0-8222-2020-2

★ **HANK WILLIAMS: LOST HIGHWAY by Randal Myler and Mark Harelik.** The story of the beloved and volatile country-music legend Hank Williams, featuring twenty-five of his most unforgettable songs. "[LOST HIGHWAY has] the exhilarating feeling of Williams on stage in a particular place on a particular night…serves up classic country with the edges raw and the energy hot…By the end of the play, you've traveled on a profound emotional journey: LOST HIGHWAY transports its audience and communicates the inspiring message of the beauty and richness of Williams' songs…forceful, clear-eyed, moving, impressive." –*Rolling Stone.* "…honors a very particular musical talent with care and energy… smart, sweet, poignant." –*NY Times.* [7M, 3W] ISBN: 0-8222-1985-9

★ **THE STORY by Tracey Scott Wilson.** An ambitious black newspaper reporter goes against her editor to investigate a murder and finds the *best* story…but at what cost? "A singular new voice…deeply emotional, deeply intellectual, and deeply musical…" –*The New Yorker.* "…a conscientious and absorbing new drama…" –*NY Times.* "…a riveting, tough-minded drama about race, reporting and the truth…" –*A.P.* "… a stylish, attention-holding script that ends on a chilling note that will leave viewers with much to talk about." –*Curtain Up.* [2M, 7W (doubling, flexible casting)] ISBN: 0-8222-1998-0

★ **OUR LADY OF 121st STREET by Stephen Adly Guirgis.** The body of Sister Rose, beloved Harlem nun, has been stolen, reuniting a group of life-challenged childhood friends who square off as they wait for her return. "A scorching and dark new comedy… Mr. Guirgis has one of the finest imaginations for dialogue to come along in years." –*NY Times.* "Stephen Guirgis may be the best playwright in America under forty." –*NY Magazine.* [8M, 4W] ISBN: 0-8222-1965-4

★ **HOLLYWOOD ARMS by Carrie Hamilton and Carol Burnett.** The coming-of-age story of a dreamer who manages to escape her bleak life and follow her romantic ambitions to stardom. Based on Carol Burnett's bestselling autobiography, *One More Time.* "…pure theatre and pure entertainment…" –*Talkin' Broadway.* "…a warm, fuzzy evening of theatre." –*BrodwayBeat.com.* "…chuckles and smiles of recognition or surprise flow naturally…a remarkable slice of life." –*TheatreScene.net.* [5M, 5W, 1 girl] ISBN: 0-8222-1959-X

★ **INVENTING VAN GOGH by Steven Dietz.** A haunting and hallucinatory drama about the making of art, the obsession to create and the fine line that separates truth from myth. "Like a van Gogh painting, Dietz's story is a gorgeous example of excess—one that remakes reality with broad, well-chosen brush strokes. At evening's end, we're left with the author's resounding opinions on art and artifice, and provoked by his constant query into which is greater: van Gogh's art or his violent myth." –*Phoenix New Times.* "Dietz's writing is never simple. It is always brilliant. Shaded, compressed, direct, lucid—he frames his subject with a remarkable understanding of painting as a physical experience." –*Tucson Citizen.* [4M, 1W] ISBN: 0-8222-1954-9

DRAMATISTS PLAY SERVICE, INC.
440 Park Avenue South, New York, NY 10016 212-683-8960 Fax 212-213-1539
postmaster@dramatists.com www.dramatists.com

NEW PLAYS

★ **INTIMATE APPAREL by Lynn Nottage.** The moving and lyrical story of a turn-of-the-century black seamstress whose gifted hands and sewing machine are the tools she uses to fashion her dreams from the whole cloth of her life's experiences. "...Nottage's play has a delicacy and eloquence that seem absolutely right for the time she is depicting..." –*NY Daily News*. "...thoughtful, affecting...The play offers poignant commentary on an era when the cut and color of one's dress—and of course, skin—determined whom one could and could not marry, sleep with, even talk to in public." –*Variety*. [2M, 4W] ISBN: 0-8222-2009-1

★ **BROOKLYN BOY by Donald Margulies.** A witty and insightful look at what happens to a writer when his novel hits the bestseller list. "The characters are beautifully drawn, the dialogue sparkles..." –*nytheatre.com*. "Few playwrights have the mastery to smartly investigate so much through a laugh-out-loud comedy that combines the vintage subject matter of successful writer-returning-to-ethnic-roots with the familiar mid-life crisis." –*Show Business Weekly*. [4M, 3W] ISBN: 0-8222-2074-1

★ **CROWNS by Regina Taylor.** Hats become a springboard for an exploration of black history and identity in this celebratory musical play. "Taylor pulls off a Hat Trick: She scores thrice, turning CROWNS into an artful amalgamation of oral history, fashion show, and musical theater..." –*TheatreMania.com*. "...wholly theatrical...Ms. Taylor has created a show that seems to arise out of spontaneous combustion, as if a bevy of department-store customers simultaneously decided to stage a revival meeting in the changing room." –*NY Times*. [1M, 6W (2 musicians)] ISBN: 0-8222-1963-8

★ **EXITS AND ENTRANCES by Athol Fugard.** The story of a relationship between a young playwright on the threshold of his career and an aging actor who has reached the end of his. "[Fugard] can say more with a single line than most playwrights convey in an entire script...Paraphrasing the title, it's safe to say this drama, making its memorable entrance into our consciousness, is unlikely to exit as long as a theater exists for exceptional work." –*Variety*. "A thought-provoking, elegant and engrossing new play..." –*Hollywood Reporter*. [2M] ISBN: 0-8222-2041-5

★ **BUG by Tracy Letts.** A thriller featuring a pair of star-crossed lovers in an Oklahoma City motel facing a bug invasion, paranoia, conspiracy theories and twisted psychological motives. "...obscenely exciting...top-flight craftsmanship. Buckle up and brace yourself..." –*NY Times*. "...[a] thoroughly outrageous and thoroughly entertaining play...the possibility of enemies, real and imagined, to squash has never been more theatrical." –*A.P.* [3M, 2W] ISBN: 0-8222-2016-4

★ **THOM PAIN (BASED ON NOTHING) by Will Eno.** An ordinary man muses on childhood, yearning, disappointment and loss, as he draws the audience into his last-ditch plea for empathy and enlightenment. "It's one of those treasured nights in the theater—treasured nights anywhere, for that matter—that can leave you both breathless with exhilaration and...in a puddle of tears." –*NY Times*. "Eno's words...are familiar, but proffered in a way that is constantly contradictory to our expectations. Beckett is certainly among his literary ancestors." –*nytheatre.com*. [1M] ISBN: 0-8222-2076-8

★ **THE LONG CHRISTMAS RIDE HOME by Paula Vogel.** Past, present and future collide on a snowy Christmas Eve for a troubled family of five. "...[a] lovely and hauntingly original family drama...a work that breathes so much life into the theater." –*Time Out*. "...[a] delicate visual feast..." –*NY Times*. "...brutal and lovely...the overall effect is magical." –*NY Newsday*. [3M, 3W] ISBN: 0-8222-2003-2

DRAMATISTS PLAY SERVICE, INC.
440 Park Avenue South, New York, NY 10016 212-683-8960 Fax 212-213-1539
postmaster@dramatists.com www.dramatists.com